OPEN AND FLEXIBLE LEARNING CENTRES

OPEN
AND FLEXIBLE
LEARNING
CENTRES

W J K Davies

National Council for Educational Technology

371.5

Published and distributed by the
National Council for Educational Technology
3 Devonshire Street, London W1N 2BA

First published 1989

ISBN 0 86184-189-1

 British Library Cataloguing in Publication Data

Davies, W. J. K. (William James Keith), *1935-*
    Open and flexible learning centres.
    1. Great Britain. Further education. Teaching methods
    I. Title II. National Council for Educational
    Technology
    374'.02'0941

    ISBN 0-86184-189-1

Printed in Great Britain by
BPCC Wheatons Ltd, Exeter

CONTENTS

PREFACE

The development of what one might call 'traditional' open learning and self-study - ie basically enhanced correspondence courses with some face-to-face tutorial guidance - has been slower than predicted and there are indications that its future development potential is limited. At the same time the development of student-centred learning approaches required by many examining bodies, together with the trend towards competence based learning, has led to a rethinking of traditional teaching and training methods.

Attention is, therefore, turning once more in both education and industry to the idea of providing in-house learning facilities in order to provide better support for self-study and to make more effective use of expensive materials. Unlike previous resource centre initiatives, however, the emphasis is now on learning rather than just provision of information.

It seems important to the writer that organisations contemplating such a learning centre approach should:

a) Think the concept through carefully before committing themselves.

b) Consider the approach as an integrative one rather than an additive one to their existing activities.

c) Avoid the danger of compartmentalisation (eg should be able to spot that 'class-teaching', 'centre' and 'home study' are not mutually exclusive concepts and each may enrich the other provision).

d) Be realistic both about the organisational requirements and the extent to which wider cost-benefits can offset some of the operational costs.

This book is intended to be a strictly practical aid to achieving these aims and also to help in the mundane tasks of setting up and running such facilities. It is suggested that, all too often, organisations do not make most use of the investment they put into flexible learning because its usefulness is preceived too narrowly. For example, it is not thought of as a possible integral element in existing courses or training programmes, or it is viewed from a fixed perspective - for example, 'Open Learning = Distance Learning'.

To help achieve a balanced view, each chapter starts with a discussion of the aspect concerned, trying to raise and answer points that keep coming up in conversations with college managements and training officers. This is followed by detailed consideration of the practical implications in each case, together with a selected list of useful references - there seems little point in reinventing wheels if perfectly satisfactory ones exist. Appendices provide some useful documentation where this does not appear to be otherwise available.

W J K Davies

1. INTRODUCTION - WHY LEARNING CENTRES?

A horse is only a camel designed by a committee - Desert proverb

Fair comment? How one sees a thing depends entirely on what one's current perceptions are and where they start from: and that appears particularly true in education where labels are thrown around with abandon but actually signify different things to different people. Indeed the differences between American and English usage pale into nothing by comparison with the difference between what educational theorists want terms to mean and what they do mean in practice. Thus the labels we shall have to use throughout this book - flexible learning, open learning, supported self-study, resource centres, learning centres, workshops - have got exactly that problem. Even two years ago, the writer would probably have tried at least to define 'open learning' in terms of its theoretical meaning: quality of choice, access, ability, support, motivation et al. For practical purposes, however, it seems more sensible to start from where most people are, and that appears to be something like the following:

Flexible learning (approach) is an up-and-coming term coined, some would say, in frustration at misinterpretation of other terms, as an 'umbrella' to cover everything. In practice it is being used to describe any attempts to make the conventional teaching process more student-oriented, so embraces the integration of individualised work of all kinds, assignment-based activities wanted by bodies such as BTEC, even the modularisation of courses and syllabi. It therefore subsumes the terms below but is too broad to be of any precise use.

Open learning on the other hand, which used to be thought of as incorporating the above elements, is now generally perceived, by institutional management at least, as learning from pre-prepared packages with or without human help of various kinds. That is, it is 'open' mainly in terms of student acess to courses which might not otherwise have been available because of small numbers, inability to attend, etc. Some powerful agencies, such as The Open College, tend to consider it as being even more narrowly defined as, effectively, the use of enhanced correspondence courses but that is not as yet a fully accepted translation.

Indeed there is currently a tendency to separate out what is called distance learning from open learning proper. Distance learning is taken as basically home study with support by a small amount of postal or face-to-face tuition and possibly a small built-in residential element. Open learning, which does to some extent subsume distance learning, is more concerned with using packages by any means but increasingly with a fair amount of on-site provision in workshops or learning centres.

Supported self-study (SS-S), which one might think was synonymous with the above, has now become virtually a coded term to describe contract-based, individualised learning schemes - usually, though not always, using assignments and guideline materials produced in-house by the sponsoring institution or groups of institutions. Organisationally it differs from the above in that it is much more likely to be thought of as applying mainly to mainstream students already enrolled on educational courses.

Conventional teaching as a term is normally used to describe traditional methods of face-to-face tuition based on class groups of economic size and homogeneous composition (typically 15:1 in FE).

In practice, none of these 'approaches' are particularly clear cut. There are few taught courses nowadays in which students at some time or other do not go off to carry out individual or small group assignments or projects. Equally the various open learning or supported self-study schemes tend, quite rightly in the writer's opinion, to concentrate on specific parts or modules rather than trying to carry out the whole task. Indeed it is an increasing move towards modularising courses which is bringing flexible approaches to the fore and which is, in turn, leading to the development of yet another term.

Mixed-mode learning, as this term is generally used, is just what it says - a blend of conventionally taught modules with others taught via open learning methods, or even a straight mix of individual packaged learning and of face-to-face tuition in small groups throughout a course. The intention may be simply to cut down contact time for a small group, thus making it economic, or it may be to offer alternative paths through a course or a training programme.

Modularisation, also, is likely to require providing institutions to make more flexible provision although, ironically, it is also in danger of compartmentalising learning more than any packaging can do. The danger is that one may end up not with modules - distinct but interlocking segments of learning - but with nodules which one might describe as totally isolated bits of learning with no thought-out links to a whole and often with no coherent size or structure. Any flexible learning approach must recognise this danger and provide ways and means to overcome it and that in turn means looking towards an overall approach to organisation and provision rather than letting small schemes develop haphazardly as need 'arises'. The latter may be cheaper and not disturb the institution so much in the short term; in the long term it is likely to be counterproductive.

If we accept the trend towards modularisation and greater flexibility, it is then the ways and means of achieving it with which we are concerned here. What are the 'new' facilities that we could have at our disposal, what are the human and organisational implications of them, and how best can we integrate them into the system - for it is suggested that, if we simply graft them on as often happens, little change will result?

In practice we have four identifiable facilities: distance learning provision; specialist subject workshops; generalist learning rooms or centres; resource areas - usually extended libraries. The latter are now widely familiar in FE, providing a range of information resources for assignment and project work and, because of the way they developed, are usually an institutional resource. The other three are much less common and, certainly in education, often form small fragmented initiatives that affect only one section of an institution, so it may be worth dwelling on them for a while.

Distance learning or, as it is sometimes called, home study provision is both the most common and least disruptive to the host organisation (which may well be why it is the most common!). Some colleges may recognise it under the trade name Flexistudy, as promoted by the National Extension College; others involved with The Open College and, in practice, even the Open University in most cases, may have it confusingly labelled open learning though it is now recognisable as a

11

distinct subset of the latter. Yet others may be running a specialist course (eg Quarrying Technology or Printing) where the potential clientele is at once small in numbers and widely scattered over the country. Industrial clients may have it identified as provision of packages which their employees work on outside the workplace. In all cases the general procedure is the same in that individuals are provided with self-study packages which they use, in general, away from the institutional premises. The institution provides a limited amount of tutorial guidance, by post, phone or face-to-face contact and may, in the case of Open University and specialist courses, build in a short residential element. They have tended to develop first because they make little demand on accommodation and because the clientele is both largely external and comparatively small so far as total institutional numbers are concerned. They can, therefore, be grafted on as a peripheral extra and expected largely to pay for themselves. The corollary is that they usually stay small scale - though, to be fair, indications are that there is actually only a limited market for this kind of approach, at least at sub-degree level.

Learning workshops (to distinguish them from conventional science or engineering labs, for example) are probably the next most common facility. They are usually single-subject (Maths and English are typical). Typically, they consist of a room or rooms fitted out for individual study, provided with a mixture of commercial and home-produced study materials and staffed largely by specialist teachers as part of their normal timetable; that is, they are expected to some extent to replace formal teaching in that subject and their clientele is therefore largely internal, composed of students already taking courses within the institution. Their flexibility lies in the provision of a wide range of materials which, together with constant staffing, allow them to respond easily to individual students' needs. At best they are an excellent resource which effectively reuses existing resources; at worst they are simply a mechanism whereby whole class groups troop in to plod through a series of sterile worksheets which may be worse than the teaching they replace. Their increasing popularity probably owes much to the fact that they are usually subject based and thus can be initiated by - and contained within - enthusiasts in one department or section. As an institutional resource, this can also be their weakness.

The third category comprises *generalised learning rooms* or centres in which, typically, one finds a wide selection of packaged materials in a range of subjects, together with some kind of student support mechanism. The materials are likely to be multi-media in many cases, since this justifies the existence of complex equipment such as videos and microcomputers and the student support may well be based on administrative staff backed up by an academic co-ordinator. Perhaps for prestige reasons, these facilities are often dignified with a name such as Open Learning Centre or Independent Learning Centre, presumably on the principle of the old 'resource centre' tag, though they rarely have the same degree of cross-institution use as, say, a library. For this reason, and also because of the expense of equipping them, they are usually seen as an additional cost and usage rarely replaces any conventional teaching as a workshop does. Hence they tend to be peripheral to the mainstream work and have a largely external clientele, which is a pity.

The use of the word 'Centre' in the title of such facilities can also cause confusion when one talks of 'learning centres' as a concept. If one talks of a learning room as a 'centre' to which students come to learn then it tends to remain something isolated from the mainstream, used only occasionally by the institution as a whole; a number of gleaming, but underused, places around the country testify to this. That will not, of course, prevent the term becoming a common perception. Yet a learning centre, in the writer's view, is something wider in scope.

Now it can be argued that this is somewhat dangerous; taking it to its logical conclusion, one can simply argue that an institution is a learning centre per se which may well be philosophically true but can lead to all sorts of resistances when trying to consider reality. So the writer would like to suggest, for our purposes, that a learning centre be thought of as more than a working room but considerably less than the whole institution; perhaps it is that part of the institution's organisation which caters for non-conventional instruction. One could define it as 'individual or student-centred learning provision contained as an identifiable element within a broader institution but serving that whole institution' - the macrocosmic rather than the microcosmic view of 'centre', so to speak! At its smallest it is a single facility of general value but that risks losing the advantages of scale. Ideally, and for the purposes of this book, we might say that a learning centre should be an entity including the following elements:

a) One or more of the facilities described above.

b) An administration and student support structure.

c) A coherent policy integrating its use into the work of its host institution so that full use is made of it both internally and externally.

So far so good; now we have our approaches and physical possibilities defined, what have we got to put in them in order to make them work? The major elements - staffing, resources, administrative structures - we will discuss later but it is worthwhile reviewing here briefly the main types of instrument that form the basis of any individualised work. Classes have teachers to provide the tuitional element - the learning information and student guidance. Learning centres, since one-to-one tuition would be impossibly expensive, must depend on structured learning materials, or packages as the current jargon has it. (To be honest, this is another instance of a misplaced term: originally a package was what it implies, the combination of materials, tuition, counselling and physical provision that made up an individual learning experience. Now it has been taken over by the marketing people to mean just the materials and, since that is the common perception, we will use that meaning here.) The intention behind all these packages is that they take over, in whole or part, the actual teaching function but, in attempting to do so, they differ widely both in concept and effectiveness.

The most comprehensive materials currently available are those designed originally as distance learning packages and it is these that one usually thinks of when open learning is mentioned. Very few even of these are fully self-contained but they normally include the following elements: a teaching text (or its media-based equivalent) which sets out to explain the learning, to guide the student through various learning tasks and to act as a general framework; some informal self-assessment checks to help the student monitor progress; one or more formal assignments to be marked and commented on by a tutor; and probably one or more externally marked attainment tests. They may be designed either to teach a specific skill or to prepare the student for an external qualification. Since they have been designed to stand alone they can be very effective indeed when used in a centre situation where constant help is available but, equally, they have some problems: many are designed as complete courses, even when modularised, so that a physical package may include much more than a student needs; the long development process makes them expensive to buy and many have been designed as 'one shot' items in which the student writes and thus prevents reuse. This is mainly because they were envisaged as being sold to home-study students whereas a centre may wish to reuse the item again and again. Fortunately suppliers are now recognising this point and are rejigging their wares.

The next most common type of package, most usually found in subject workshops, is the course or module based on sets of worksheets of one kind or another. These are often locally produced, or acquired from another institution that has produced them. Their intention is usually much the same as that of the packages described above in that they set out to replace some of the teaching element in a conventional course but they tend to be broken up into much shorter units and to require much more teacher guidance and control. Most are, again, designed to be expendable but since they cost less to produce and get dog-eared anyway this is not such a disadvantage. Their main disadvantages are a tendency to be repetitive and boring and an exaggerated confidence in their authors as to their effectiveness.

Lastly there are the various types of assignment materials particularly associated with supported self-study schemes. These again vary widely in form and content but in general are skeletal guidelines to learning tasks, the learning feedback coming mainly from interaction with the tutoring staff. They are, of course, the easiest and cheapest to produce but the penalty you pay - if it is a penalty - is that they require much more human support to be effective. If the student numbers and teaching resources are available, and if the teaching approach required is an enquiry-based one, then they are very useful. Otherwise one needs to consider carefully their advantages and disadvantages.

To sum up, materials available range from almost self-contained items through teaching packs requiring various degrees of teacher intervention to skeleton guidelines. The danger with concentrating attention on any one of them is that the 'openness' of the learning situation can quickly become illusory. The wider the prospective audience for a learning centre or workshop, the wider the variety of learning materials it needs - and a narrow concentration, equally, can sharply narrow its effectiveness.

Implications for the Institution

The implications for any institution, whether educational or commercial, wishing to investigate learning centres are simple but vital. What does the institution hope to *do* - to add on a useful facility that may attract new custom unable to use its existing courses; to embed innovatory techniques within its mainstream work; to provide a focus for changing its staff attitudes? To impress its neighbours. . . ? Does it want a combination of these? Careful consideration of all the options now that increasing information is available should prove productive; Topsy-led innovation is acceptable while it is at the leading edge but we are now past that point so far as individual learning facilities are concerned.

Useful References

Coombe Lodge Working Papers: the FE Staff College at Blagdon periodically issues working papers considering educational issues. Inevitably they date quite quickly so no specific references are given here.

Davies, W J K, *Alternatives to Class Teaching in Schools and Colleges* (Guidelines 9), CET, 1980. A few parts of this are now dated but much of the practical advice is still useful.

Davies, W J K, *Towards Autonomy in Learning: process or product?* (Occasional Paper 12), CET, 1987. A critical survey of the current position of learner-centred approaches and their possible future roles.

Implementing Open Learning in Local Authority Institutions, FEU, 1988. A very useful document to initiate institutional thinking.

Race, P, *Flexible Approaches to Training,* CET, 1987. A useful introduction to making training more trainee-centred, with all that implies.

2. LEARNING CENTRES - THE DETAILED CONCEPT

'If it were done when 'tis done, then 'twere well it were done quickly'
- Macbeth (though he was probably thinking more in terms
of changing personnel rather than attitudes)

'To be, or not to be - that is the question?' - Hamlet
(the remainder of this soliloquy is very relevant as reflecting
the thoughts of many principals and training managers
when confronted with proposals for innovation!)

The introduction suggested that we now recognise a number of discrete approaches to what one might call 'other than conventional teaching', even if we sometimes have different ideas about what each term means. Perhaps we might now go further and think of an institution's provision as being, effectively, divided into conventional (ie class-based teaching) and non-conventional (which includes all other approaches). Granted, one can argue that such a division is far too abrupt; there is a spectrum which runs all the way from individual learning to group-based formal instruction and the great mass of college or training organisation provision forms a large bulge in the middle; most taught courses, as already noted, include some assignment work these days and there is a tendency for even the most student-oriented work to include formal elements. From the organisational and conceptual point of view, however, the broad distinction is probably valid or at least one can divide the spectrum broadly into three - taught classes; individualised learning of various types; and mixed-mode courses which combine the two approaches deliberately to cover certain situations.

Just what the increasing pressure for modularisation of courses in mainstream education and training will do in this respect is not really clear at present. Most likely, in the writer's opinion, we shall move increasingly towards what one might call a mixable mode approach. However cost-effective the traditional 'batch-production' element of class teaching may be, there will be sufficient pressure from falling numbers and demand for flexible entry and exit times to make it less easy to run and less popular with clients. There will, therefore, be a need at least to deal with smallish groups and with situations in which, although

17

there may be a reasonable number of students, they come in a trickle throughout the year. Thus, if 15:1 is the economic ratio for providing formal classes, we have to look at different ways of obtaining the same effectiveness in the emerging situation. Add to this a tendency for many clients to require shortish bouts of specific training (for example in adult retraining) rather than standard qualification courses, and this needs not just a tacking on of the odd workshop or home study scheme but a rethink of how total provision can be made more flexible. To sum up, perhaps, a prospective client should have the choice of the options (or combinations of them) shown in *Figure 1*. Certainly the institution needs to have such options available so that it can adjust its provision according to circumstances. There is likely always to be a need for formal teaching where numbers permit but equally it is likely to be more often an element in a mixed course rather than its mainstay - for instance, common cores of a variety of related courses, with the optional elements covered by other means - and even the common cores may, at any one time, include students at different stages of their work.

Now hopefully we may be able to use the learning centre concept to help solve this dilemma but if we are to do so, we need to have a clear idea of what that concept is and, in the writer's opinion at least, it is not what too often eventuates in reality. In reality, the first thing that attracts many people to the term 'learning centre' is not the idea of flexible provision but the vision of rooms full of gleaming equipment and brightly coloured packages used by a constant succession of intelligent, motivated people who require little or no attention - what might be called the high street retailer's view of educational life. Equally the epitaph for many such 'centres' is the reality of unsuitable accommodation, underused except perhaps as an overflow teaching space and with most of its expensive resources slowly gathering dust.

This, as already suggested, seems to be the result of a too narrow perception of what is needed to resolve our overall dilemma; potted seedlings do not bear much fruit until they have been planted out and assimilated into the total garden. Let us consider, instead, the idea that a 'learning centre' describes what can result from combining, as one, all those parts of the institutional organisation that look after the non-standard or non-conventional aspects of learning provision - short

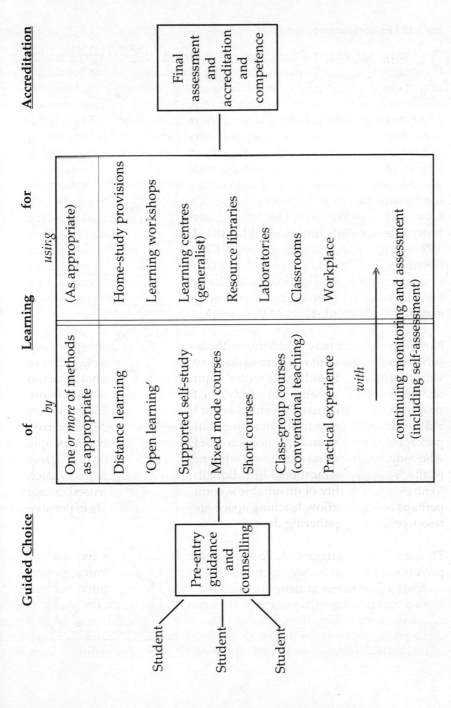

Figure 1 - Desirable Options for Learners

□ Central function   ○ Facility
C = control   S = service   Co = co-ordination
L = liaision/communication

INSTITUTION

A. Fully centralised

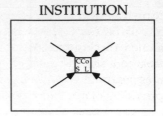

B. Central control/dispersed facilities

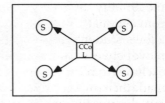

C. Central co-ordination/dispersed facilities

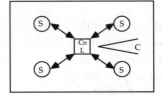

D. As above but with direct links

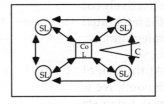

E. Disseminated system

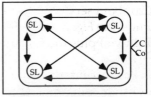

Figure 2 - Possible Organisation Models for 'Learning Centres'

courses, learning workshops, home study, seminars, the lot. After all, any of these will probably benefit from being linked with the others, let alone with class based provision; too often again they work in blinkered isolation: short course organisers don't think of using self-study modules; learning workshops do not consider what they might offer to the providers of specialist seminars needing practical work. . . etc, etc.

In such cases, the physical concept of a learning centre becomes at once the totality of the student-oriented facilities (including the non-conventional course structures) plus the organisational element that allows students or their sponsors to pick appropriate modes and to move between them as circumstances require. One might, oddly enough, exclude from this one element that 'non-conventional' initiatives have made their own because it was often previously ignored - the institution's initial counselling and assessment of student need facility, since that is basic to all types of provision and is now being recognised as such.

If we accept the general concept, however, let us also note that we must examine both aspects: facilities, except very limited ones, are of little use without an organisation to integrate them. Equally the organisation concept is no use without a range of facilities to act as its practical arm. The greater part of this book, therefore, will be on the problems of organising such facilities within an institution in such a way that they are effectively combined but please, while reading it, hang on to the idea that the integrated whole is always greater than the sum of its parts. It is this integration, and its organisation, that will be examined now.

At the risk of driving into a frenzy all those who hate diagrams and models, we will now examine the main models that an institution can use. Let us start from the axiom that organisation and integration are all about control and communication and, if physical facilities are involved, also about service. There is a spectrum of opportunities as shown rather crudely in *Figure 2*. Briefly, assuming that each circle represents physical facility(s) plus the functions noted, we have the following:

a) Totally centralised, both organisationally and physically, with clients and staff coming to it for assistance and service. This certainly offers economies of scale provided that the initial financing can be found but can easily become cumbersome and monolithic.

b) A variant with a strong central control element but with its practical components - workshops, learning rooms, distance study schemes and other facilities - sited wherever they best seem to meet the needs of the institution. This is a pattern frequently found in industrial training departments where there is a hierarchical structure and where the training needs of the company can be clearly identified.

c) A scheme in which the practical facilities are dispersed but still linked solely through a co-ordinating organisation - which may influence and serve rather than control their activities but which does ensure 'total' knowledge of what is happening at any one time. This is likely to lead to some duplication of administrative and staffing arrangements because of the semi-autonomous nature of the individual facilities and may, thus, be more costly than the first two.

d) As for (c) but with the organisation modified to allow direct links between the various facilities and between them and their clients. This clearly allows greater speed of response but is likely to be less generally effective unless it includes a system for ensuring that the central co-ordinating function is kept informed of direct transactions.

e) A totally decentralised network in which the various elements relate directly to each other without external guidance or control - or at best by some form of consultative group. This certainly has attractions in minimising the 'central' element which can be perceived as non-productive but it may result in a less effective total provision, especially in the early stages. Ironically it is only when the concept has been fully integrated in the institution's work that this scheme comes into its own as the need for central co-ordination lessens.

Obviously in each case, the central function, where it exists, can be carried out either by a person (or team of people) or by a committee, or by some combination of the two. The question is, which of these or their variants would best serve the needs of an institution? The easy way out is to say that there is no one answer; the important thing is to have all the relevant information about them so that each institution can judge what is best in its particular circumstances. On current experience, some variant of (b), (c) or (d) seems to be offering the best compromise between flexibility and control for new initiatives, provided the elements genuinely are linked together at institutional level. Even here, however, the exact pattern must depend on what exactly the institution wishes to achieve.

Implications for the Organisation of Learning Centres

The implications of the above are considerable. First and foremost evidence suggests that there are really only two alternative courses for an institution to adopt if it wants to develop flexible learning seriously. Either it keeps the whole matter low-key, allowing individual initiatives to grow and develop as chance permits, or it takes the wider concept on board as soon as possible to obtain the long term planning advantages. The first has the advantages that it is comparatively inexpensive, that it may well fit in better with emerging staff attitudes, that it tends to follow rather than try to anticipate demand - and hence is not so likely to be underused at first; the corresponding disadvantages are that it becomes much harder to restructure such initiatives if the need arises and that they may make wasteful use of resources.

The second course of action has the advantages that it allows strategic planning, and that it can economise overall on resources though it may actually be more expensive in detail. It does, however, imply a total institutional commitment from the start with all that that implies in terms of reallocation of resources, redeployment of personnel and changes in attitude; a very few colleges and some large firms have grasped this nettle but even their initiatives are still in the formative stage and the implications are rarely grasped by visitors. (For example, the workshops at Bradford & Ilkley College are often cited as an excellent example of 'how to do it' but how many people realise the period of time that was needed to arrive at the present position?)

Unless an institution is prepared for all the physical upheavals that the second course would demand, perhaps the most preferable route is, indeed, a compromise in which the overall strategic framework is devised and a co-ordinating organisation set up but in which facilities are developed as the need for them arises - but developed within the overall plan with all the communication and control advantages that implies. This does at least give the institution a touchstone against which to judge proposals and to influence their development while keeping response time fairly short.

As to the exact organisation, the institution must decide for itself. For industrial use the writer suggests that (b) above is likely to be effective, while in education (c) - which will eventually drift into (d) or (e) if it works - is probably the best since it helps to ensure integration while minimising empire-building.

Useful References
The fact is that currently there are few useful references on the total concept of learning centres - hence this book. The following, however, do give helpful information about specific components of any such system:

Davies, W J K, *Alternatives to Class Teaching in Schools and Colleges* (Guidelines 9), CET, 1980.

Lewis, R, *Open Learning in Action* (Open Learning Guide 1), CET, 1984.

Rowlands, N and S, *Into Open Learning*, Open Learning Systems Ltd, 1986.

Thorpe, M and Grugeon, D (eds), *Open Learning for Adults*, Longman, 1987.

Twining, J (ed), *Open Learning for Technicians*, Stanley Thornes, 1982.

3. FINANCING LEARNING CENTRES

'Annual income 105p, annual expenditure 100p,
result: happiness. Annual income 95p, expenditure 100p,
result: Vice Principal panics' - Mr Micawber updated

It may seem a little arbitrary, if not actually sordid, to start by discussing money rather than ideals but everything comes down to finance in the end - and especially with a learning centre because usually it is seen as an extra, an improvement on existing provision rather like extending the library, so that no company division or college department feels it actually has to divert resources to the common good. The $64,000 question is 'Should it be?'.

The concept of self-financing (or somebody else financing) appears to have sprung initially from the idea of open learning as an additional, and often 'full cost', way of providing adult learning programmes when for some reason people are disobliging enough not to come forward in sufficient numbers to make conventional provision viable; in educational circles, the argument (tacitly) appears to be that if the provider is put to inconvenience, the client must pay if he or she still wants the goods, while industry has tended simply to follow the trend because of the way 'open learning' has been promoted nationally. Yet even here we are inconsistent because internal workshops tend, somehow, to be largely assimilated within the existing system and can be made available on a fill-in basis. Take your Maths course by distance learning and you pay a high cost for materials plus (for any adequate tutorial help) more than you would pay for a class; do it by coming into a Maths workshop and you may well get away with a normal class fee which suddenly includes use of the materials and widespread access to help. Equally, if as a trainee you attend an individual learning facility at a training centre, you frequently do it at no overt expense to your work section and in the firm's time. This seems to be because such facilities are often conceived initially as being mainly of use to internal students and redeploy existing staff rather than bringing in extra ones. Is there a lesson here?

Furthermore, education at least, as a whole, has not seriously yet begun to grasp the financial complexities of 'roll-on/roll off' schemes or provision of help on demand. . . or of interspersing individualised modules with small-group teaching, so you may get widely differing offers within the same establishment. Is there a lesson for us here also? It is interesting that training organisations, where they have decided to set up centres, have done the thing properly; it may be argued that they have a captive audience, but the centre is usually financed on its predicted value to the organisation rather than on student costings and the cost/benefits are taken into consideration. In education, college libraries are already run on this principle and some learning workshops follow it tacitly in that internal students are not charged extra while external ones attract only a marginal cost.

It must be admitted that, because of all these factors, and because of the way in which 'OL' developed, it is very difficult to provide any sensible guidance on general costings for learning centres in education; there are many guides but they are, in general, attempts to fit individuals effectively doing distance learning or self-study into the framework of an existing finance system based on calculations derived from 15:1 class teaching. Perhaps we might better start by querying whether we should be thinking initially of *costing* or *financing* such major shifts of existing practice.

Financing and costing, the writer sees as two different ends of the spectrum. You can cost a given course of action and charge to cover (finance) it from the start without additional investment if it is a marginal activity. Conversely, you can finance a given course of action and try to ensure that use rises to cover those costs which you have identified as extra, taking into account any cost-benefits that accrue to existing provision. Experience to date indicates that the first approach is long, painful and rarely becomes more than peripheral. The second appears to require either an identified need (eg workshops) or an act of faith or some source of investment. Yet surely in any business venture it is normal to capitalise it first and to provide any infrastructure that may be necessary to make it work.

As a crude analogy, take the case of a service station owner who decides to extend into the business of actually repairing vehicles. He *could*, of course, wait for a customer and then contract with a mechanic he knows just to repair that vehicle, providing tools, materials, etc specially for the job each time and then throwing them away afterwards. He doesn't have to risk capital but is unlikely to get very far. . . What he is more likely to do is to spend capital on either extending or altering his premises, equip them suitably and either hire competent staff or retrain some of his existing ones - he recognises that the physical plant in itself is not sufficient. Then he offers a competitive and reliable service, hopefully getting work from both existing and new customers. He may go bankrupt if he has misjudged the market but he certainly has a better chance of making his new venture work. If he also happens to be running his own hire fleet which the new facility can service instead of having to contract out, the investment becomes even more viable and he may be able to accept quite low levels of external trade while it develops. You see the point of course: institutions running ad hoc provision are taking the first course of action with predictable results; even those who do see the need for capitalisation are often unwilling to take the logical step of actually manning the facility for their own benefit in advance of demand. Admittedly, the staffing, both for education and industry, probably comes out of a different budget, and one that is more difficult than capital to manipulate, but it still needs to be provided for a full service.

There are ways of overcoming these problems but not a lot of existing guidance, as we noted before. It may, therefore, be worth backtracking a little and examining the problems from first principles - and if this is teaching grandparents to suck eggs, so be it.

Let us start by looking at the problem from the costing angle, then discussing ways of finally considering the pricing implications.

Consider that any training or educational activity starting from an existing base has three main provider 'costs' attached (even if subsidised, the principle still applies). These are:

a) infrastructure costs
b) tuition costs
c) materials costs (including consumables such as file paper).

27

In conventional FE class provision, the student fee charged presumably attaches itself mainly to (a) and (b) though even then most of the infrastructure costs are normally assimilated apart from staffing overheads - and even these are subsidised. (c) is normally borne by the student but is rarely significant except in practically based subjects (eg engineering or cookery) or higher-level academic courses where text and reference books become expensive; even then, in the latter case, some cost can be recouped since the books are reusable. Thus the main identifiable cost, on which student charges are based, is that of staffing the tuition element which is 'covered' by calculating a minimum student/tutor ratio - currently of 15:1 - and assuming that lower numbers are not viable unless special circumstances apply.

Now open learning - as home study - has grown up in that framework and the home study student therefore suffers in all ways: the costing contortions needed to operate within the existing system mean that, even for the same charge as a class student, he gets very little human contact yet, in order to acquire the materials theoretically replacing some of that contact, he has to pay all over again - for it is the structured teaching element in such materials that makes them intrinsically more expensive than an equivalent textbook and the need to have exclusive use of them that leads an institution to sell such material on. The result in practice tends to be a second-best experience with only the theoretical advantages of 'at one's own place, at one's own pace' to recommend it. There have been various attempts somehow to provide the tuition element more economically, such as by using group seminars, 'surgeries' and case-load systems but these have largely been designed for the provider's benefit (ie to reduce cost rather than extend student support) and most have been predicated on the 'home-study for individuals' basis. Very little indeed has been done to try to rationalise the, often very heavy, materials cost to the client. In effect, because this is still responding to requests rather than trying to anticipate them, the situation tends to be one of considerable underinvestment which, in turn, fails to produce effective results.

Now while not trying to decry the home study movement, the thesis of this book is that the learning centre/workshop approach is more likely to provide a viable base from which a wide variety of initiatives, including home study, can operate. Furthermore, all experience to date shows that this cannot be done on a retrospective costing basis. To have a chance of working, it must be adequately financed in advance and its running expenses then calculated to meet that proportion of costs which is judged necessary (this, as we shall see, may well be complicated by the fact that extensive use is likely to be made of the facility by internal students who cannot be directly charged. Does the 'centre' make a service charge against their sponsors?). It is in this area of prior financing that little published evidence is available since the more advanced educational users have often achieved their ends indirectly while the visible industrial ones are mainly high-tech and specialised (cf Austin-Rover), the companies concerned reckoning that the benefits outweigh the costs incurred.

Working from first principles then, what are the major elements of financing and their implications? Inevitably they are those which incur the main costs - infrastructure, tuition and materials but with emphasis on the first and last since tuition is essentially a running cost. Indeed its importance in the scheme depends on whether the 'centre' or workshop is seen as a peripheral extra or a means of embedding changing techniques within the maintream of education and training. If it is the former, then one has the same problems as with home study; if it is the latter, however, then almost by definition staffing resources become to some extent available. Staff who are no longer teaching, either because their 'class' does x per cent of its work in the workshop or is not running because of small numbers, can, in the right circumstances, be used to man the new facilities in a support and tutorial role. This is easier for a single subject workshop than for a generalist one but it can be done (see chapter 4). Nevertheless, it may be necessary to schedule additional staff in to cover all desired periods and so there are clear financing implications. Similarly there are implications because it is necessary to have the facilities manned whether or not student use eventuates. It is not possible to give precise cost guidelines on this point because the need for 'tuition-level' staff (ie qualified teachers or trainers) will vary widely (see chapter 9 for a discussion of this).

On infrastructure financing we can be much clearer. Infrastructure costs for a learning centre include both non-recurring and recurring elements.

The former are those relating to the establishment of the physical plant; the latter are the costs of organising and administering it, including provision of reception, non-academic supervision, etc. It is important to note that they are not unique; almost any participative learning environment has to include them - a science laboratory needs its special furniture, equipment and technician help as does an engineering workshop or, for that matter, a library. The difference is that such environments were normally built in as a matter of course when the institution or training department was first set up and were recognised traditionally as areas requiring such special provision. In making a case for financing, or in allocating resources itself, the sponsoring institution has to recognise that a similar investment is now needed.

In this respect the writer's experience is that organisations, if they want the facility, can usually find the minimum resources to allocate and adapt basic accommodation - though here again it is easier in a subject workshop since that often replaces class activity and thus frees space. They or their paymasters also tend to be able, albeit reluctantly, to find capital for at least a modicum of the media equipment - microcomputers, videos, etc - to outfit the physical presence. What does tend to happen is that this aspect is skimped somewhat, with long-term consequences. The other two aspects, supervisory staffing and materials provision, are much more often neglected yet we should emphasise that they are an essential part of any financing; just as a library needs counter assistants or a laboratory needs technicians who can help with many routine tasks and queries, so a generalist learning centre needs administrative/ reception staff on duty whenever it is open so any calculations must include this. In addition, as a new facility, a generalist centre or multi-workshop scheme will need someone actually to drive it, perhaps more than one post if the facility is to be of any size.

With regard to materials, the same applies. In our analogy, no one would expect the garage proprietor to equip his repair shop with two spanners and a hammer or a library to start with bare shelves and buy in books as students requested them. Equally, to provide a credible service, a learning centre of any kind must have a basic stock of learning resource materials, both reusable (which are, of course, most economic) and at least selected consumable items (see chapter 6 for a discussion of these).

Educational organisations in particular are often reluctant to commit funds to this but any reasonable centre should expect to spend some £4,000 - £5,000 on initial stock at 1989 prices; otherwise it is likely to turn away more clients than it helps. Exactly the same, incidentally, should apply to subject workshops. There is a strong tendency to concentrate on one series of assignment materials - sometimes home produced, sometimes bought in - without considering that different students may need different approaches - and, too, without considering that the recurrent costs may multiply frighteningly (both in reprographics and in replacement once the originators leave!).

Lastly we come to the thorny question of student charges. Frankly, in education, so far as internal students are concerned, the writer can see no alternative to treating the facility as industrial units usually do and educational libraries do: as a service which is part of the institution's provision and therefore freely available to bona fide students without extra charge. It may require the institution to 'top-slice' an amount from its budget before distributing anything to sections rather than charge user sections retrospectively, because the latter course of action discourages rather than encourages use. It will also require the institution to take responsibility for manning the centre during working hours if it tries to claw back some of the cost. The manning may be undertaken by redeploying staff as institutional needs change or, once a pattern of use is established, by 'levying' on departmental or specialist staffing in proportion to their use of the facility. This latter course does have the advantage of ensuring that appropriate specialist cover is available at a range of times and also of encouraging internal use so that the departments get value for their contribution!

For external students (that is those not using the facility as an integral part of another course they attend) the position is somewhat more contentious. If the overall funding has been accepted as suggested above, then they can be regarded as providing marginal income and a number of LEAs accept that the equivalent evening course fee should be charged so that they are not disadvantaged. Others, however, insist on full cost course recovery which, together with the materials cost often charged under 'traditional OL' conditions usually makes the cost prohibitive. The writer would suggest that the workshop/centre

31

approach provides opportunity for a fresh way of examining such charges and the implications are discussed below.

Financial Implications of Workshops and Learning Centres
To recap, the financial implications of setting up an effective facility are quite clear. It is an expensive business and really needs to be recognised as being on the same level of magnitude as establishing, say, a library on a satellite site, or setting up and equipping a new science laboratory. This is something which large firms and private training providers venturing into the area usually have no difficulty in grasping but, there, resources usually follow the will to do something. In the prevailing financial circumstances, educational institutions tend to try and build up 'by the back door' funding a piece at a time and always trying to follow rather than lead demand. That may be because current percep-tions of traditional OL emphasise its cost and the small demand that follows but nevertheless the attitude exists.

This may at times be inevitable but, even so, the institution concerned should recognise the financial advantages of having a strategic plan to match suggested initiatives against and to build successful ones into. Furthermore, in many colleges especially, one can nowadays find four or five quite separate pockets of 'open learning' - a Maths workshop here, a home study scheme there, a flexibly run engineering course somewhere else - which have sprung up on a minimum funding basis and which do not speak to each other; one even knows cases where they do not know each other exists. Now, if the total college situation is analysed, it often becomes apparent that the overall use of such re-sources is wasteful. Usage in any one does not justify proper manning; there are driblets of administrative assistance in each; there are overlaps which were not recognised. This is not flexible learning, it is uneconomic chauvinism in all too many cases. The first major implication, if funding is tight, is therefore to look very hard at the advantages of concentration of effort. Even if physical facilities are separate, are there areas where common servicing would economise (eg administrative support)? By combining physical facilities could one member of staff provide cover that currently requires two? Would a common contact point help? If an institution is already committed to such initiatives this is desirable; if it is starting afresh then, the writer suggests, it is mandatory.

So much for setting-up costs: individual costs per institution differ so much depending on the circumstances that it is not possible to give definite figures but the capital or minor works budget must certainly allow enough to provide for converting and furnishing to a comfortable standard a space (or spaces) sufficient for the student numbers envisaged plus administrative accommodation. If external customers are considered important, it is also desirable that a separate dedicated telephone line be installed.

Having actually provided the physical basis, including any equipment (see chapter 5), the workshop or centre will need an initial set of materials, just as a library needs books or a laboratory needs raw materials. A centre or workshop approach implies that many clients will actually work on site, using materials held by the centre. This is not only good educational practice in that it concentrates resources but is probably the most economical way of using expensive items. The first implication is that any centre will need an initial, comprehensive set of materials to act as its stock in trade. A subject workshop may well need multiple copies of a restricted range, a generalist one is likely to need a wide range of single copies. Either way, an investment of £4,000 - £5,000 at 1989 prices will be needed to provide a basis and this may be more if multiple copies of the more expensive packages are needed.

If the above premises are accepted, the institution will also need to accept the recurrent costs of co-ordinating and administering the work. These will certainly involve provision of either a single person at a senior level, or an allocation of time to a group (or both) and chapter 4 discusses this. The point to note here is that such work is also administration-intensive and any provision must also allow for costing in administrative staff at a reasonable level (HAY level 4 or 5 should be the miniumum).

Running Costs and Student Charges
The first problem is to establish what costs are to be taken into account. The writer has argued above that the basic co-ordination and administration costs, together with heating, lighting and other recurring overheads, should really be accepted by the institution as part of its general provision; the only exception might be when a facility is envisaged as being wholly for external clients and thus becomes a true cost centre.

Otherwise it is reasonable to argue that the base costs are assumed by the institution as a quid pro quo for some of the cost-benefits realised through use of such facilities by internal students/trainees as an integral part of their courses. If an institution does not do this then it will have to make a calculation as to the hourly costs attributable to infrastructure and modify the formula below accordingly.

This, as mentioned above, leaves us with the need at least to determine the direct running costs which, effectively, are those of tuition and materials depreciation. In this respect the cost of a student using the centre (ie working there) for one hour can be established by use of a simple formula (though the exact definition of the variables may be more difficult!). The formula is:

$$\frac{M + (CD)}{C}$$

where M = the direct manning cost; C = a chosen proportion of the notional student capacity; D = a materials depreciation element.

Note that the divisor is a proportion of notional student capacity because, just as an airline cannot calculate its fares on selling 100% seating, so a centre or workshop is unlikely to be completely full all the time.

Fine, so what about the variables? Given that many problems are low-level ones, experience has shown that, with students responsible for their own learning, a ratio of 1:12 or 1:15 is attainable, so that for every twelve or fifteen student work stations, one tutor/supervisor is allocated. This can be varied to institutional requirements but 1:12 is used in the example below.

The materials depreciation charge is more difficult since we do not have enough evidence to quote a firm figure and since even reusable materials vary so widely; some paper based packages will scarcely survive a couple of months of extensive use, some CBT ones are still usable after the same number of years. Suggestions for this therefore range from

£0.00, on the basis that in-centre materials are part of the basic provision, to a fixed proportion of package cost irrespective of nature (not easy since it involves differential charging) to an average, often token, sum. The only exact way is to monitor actual costs over a period and then use the results. From experience, a notional sum of £0.25 per use/hour, to include provision of non-consumable materials only, or £0.50 per use/ hour to include consumables such as workbooks or worksheets, seem to be about right.

The 'seat break-even' factor is certainly another variable but one more susceptible of resolution. Between 60% and 75% occupancy is reason- able to expect once the facility is in full use and the latter is taken in the example below.

Let us, then, take a 12-place workshop requiring one member of staff at, say, £15.00 per hour including on-costs (which is a little generous for educational part-time staff at the time of writing). Substituting the suggested values in the formula gives:

$$(15 + 2.25) \text{ divided by } 9 = 1.92$$

giving a notional student cost of just under £2.00 per student per hour. Note that this assumes each student uses a pack for the hour he or she is in the centre and is able to call on help as required from centre staff. Clearly the exact allocation of variables can vary widely and note that there may be economies of scale. In a generalist centre with twice the above capacity, it might well be sensible to have one tutor and one admin assistant on duty. With the latter at, say, £5.00 per hour, the student cost, assuming the other variables remain static, reduces to

$$(20 + 4.5) \text{ divided by } 18 = 1.36$$

Some very large capacity facilities, with 100 places or more, have been able to reduce the manning cost element even further.

Conversely, increasing the tuition cover or accepting a low occupancy rates pushes the marginal cost per student upwards while increasing the number of students per supervisor will correspondingly lower it -

another illustration of why such facilities need to be integrated, to maximise use if the cost benefits equation is to be acceptable. It is obvious that this formula can be used to ascertain the actual cost to a sponsoring department, or company section, of having a student in the centre rather than being taught elsewhere, but its main utility is to establish the marginal costs of servicing external students in order to allow a realistic charge to be fixed.

It should also be noted that this cost is that for a student working in the centre. It does not cover the following possible additional costs:

a)   Any extra guidance, counselling or tutorial help required.

b)   Any material (other than consumable) which the student wishes to take away from the centre to work on elsewhere.

These may be considered as optional costs which, for internal students, are normally insignificant: the guidance, etc is likely to be provided as part of their main study programme and materials can, reasonably, be loaned on a library basis against a deposit if needed. The writer has operated both systems satisfactorily.

For external students, the additional costs vary: tuition support may be via a 'surgery' arrangement additional to normal centre manning, in which case a sum per hour can be calculated on a similar type of formula, for example:

direct manning cost divided by notional students per session

(ie if a tutor could 'handle' 5 students per hour, the individual cost would be £3.00 per session, whether as a seminar or individual attention for a shorter time. Bear in mind that this is not a main source of tuition for a centre or workshop student but only occasional extra help.) Alternatively any of the available formulae for home study tutoring could be utilised.

Materials cost again depends on policy more than rationale. A short-term loan might be free or a nominal sum; possession of a package for the duration of a 'course' can be done either by selling-on (expensive) or by some form of renting, typically against a deposit. Again there is little statistical evidence on which to base such costs but, from experience, packages that are takable away (ie do not require specialised equipment) can stand up to about five or six cycles of use. Thus a rental charge of about 20% of package cost should enable one to amortise and replace the rental stock provided its content is stable; if the latter may change, perhaps because qualifications change, then a higher charge may be needed to offset the likely shorter use period.

All the above calculations, of course, determine only basic marginal costs; the only 'profit margin' built in occurs if the centre occupancy rate exceeds its calculated proportion. The institution therefore has to decide whether it wishes to make a notional surplus to provide income against future needs or, indeed, to build in some of the additional costs quoted above (for example, increasing the staff-student ratio to 1:6 in a specialised training facility with 60% occupancy would give a marginal cost of £4.00 per student per hour, spread among all students rather than just those who demanded extra support.

How does all this relate to student charges? The implication is that, if an institution wants to cover its direct running costs, the effective marginal cost per student for a typical workshop or centre attendance is probably between £1.50 and £2.50 per hour at 1989 prices, and in that case this is probably the rate that should be considered on a 'fill-in basis' (ie if the facility is not a cost-centre). There may, however, well be arguments for discounting charges, for example:

a) For a series for sessions booked in advance which guarantee income and cut down on administration; this is after all effectively what is done in a class fee and, for FE at least, the result would come very close to the charge for a one-term evening class.

b) If considerable use is made of the facility by the institution for internal students or trainees. In that case a proportion at least of the manning costs and materials depreciation should effectively be debitable to the institution as part of the cost-benefits.

In such cases the actual student charge is, therefore, significantly lower. Indeed some FE institutions then work the charge on the basis of the current vocational course rate (about 55p/hr average at time of writing). If to this is added a materials depreciation element as formulated above, the resulting student charge would approximate to 80p/hr excluding consumables or £1.05 including them.

At that point, policy comes in. The institution can either charge an hourly rate for each visit (spreads the load but increases administration) or issue some form of season ticket. Again this can simply be calculated on the hourly rate for x hours - allowing, say, 24 hours during a term which, at 80p/hr, would come to £19.20 - or the ticket can be of unlimited validity for a given period (eg 12 weeks) with an overall price calculated on likely use. In the writer's experience, that latter is better for public relations and usually averages out effectively but, in any case, the institution can, and should, monitor use to see how its predictions are working out. It can then revise its policy to suit.

The formulae can, however, help for other purposes. Indeed calculations of this nature are most useful when considering differential charging, between individuals and sponsored clients for example. While individuals are effectively subsidised, certainly in conventional education, for corporate clients there is a tendency to charge 'what the market will bear'; it is suggested that, in a workshop or centre this can be directly related to the pattern of service provided. Individual students responsible for their own learning may well have the motivation and indirect support to cope with 'normal' conditions as laid down above. Where an educational or training institution in effect contracts with a client to ensure success in specific training (errors and omissions excepted) it may well feel the need to cost in a higher level of support, possibly a set of materials, probably a contribution towards its overhead costs and also a profit margin. A typical figure, at 1989 prices, comes to between £6.50 and £7.50 an hour to which may be added materials charges where appropriate. The formulae above should at least enable this to be justifiable rather than arbitrary.

Useful References
Most of the available references are predicated on a 'traditional' home study view of open learning. Bearing that in mind, the following are of value:

Birch, D W and Cuthbert, R E, *Costing Open Learning in Further Education*, CET, 1981. A useful guide to some of the problems, although concentrating on 'traditional' open learning.

Crabb, G A, *Costing Open Learning* (provisional title), NCET, forthcoming early 1990. This pack will be a practical working guide to assist in the accurate costing of open and innovative learning.

Ely Resource and Technology Centre, *Costing and Pricing Learning Materials*, CET, 1983. An invaluable practical guide to the real costs of producing learning materials.

Fielden, J and Pearson, P K, *Costing Educational Practice*, CET, 1978. A practical guide to undertaking cost analyses and understanding costing.

4. PROVISION, MANAGEMENT AND USE OF STAFFING RESOURCES

'I don't know exactly how we developed; like Topsy it "just growed" '
- Any anonymous head of department or training manager
trying to explain an innovation that has got out of hand

Very few of us now remember who the original Topsy was but the saying is still familiar as indicating the process of something that was not planned but just evolved pragmatically from an initial stimulus. In many institutions, both educational and industrial, the current approach to staffing facilities of the sort we are discussing can best be described as being pragmatic or 'Topsy-led'; a subject workshop may well simply have existing staff redeployed from other teaching modes which its approach replaces; a brand new 'learning centre' may result in a special appointment who is often expected to be all things to all men; an initiative funded from outside may furnish short term staff with only vague consideration of the future. On the other hand, 'traditional' OL of the home study type frequently depends on raising short-term, part-time staffing, following rather than anticipating demand and thus largely unpredictable, while, all too often, internal initiatives depend on either a minimal amount of remission 'to develop materials' etc, or even on the goodwill of staff with no extra time allocated at all.

To be fair, in such instances, the initial staff often choose to get involved because they are enthusiastic about innovation but that needs to be recognised as only an initial phase. Sooner or later, if the initiative is successful, the work resulting has to be assimilated within the total work of the institution and staffing has to be put on a proper footing... at which point the two main problems of such an approach become apparent: the staff involved may have been chosen for purely pragmatic reasons (light timetables, personal interest, etc) and may not actually be those most suitable to carry the innovation forward; the current gradings of staff involved may have been determined by their previous role and, again, may not be those most appropriate to future plans. Indeed, since they are likely to be more junior than the new role requires, such staff often do not have much institutional clout and are likely to get very frustrated

41

in consequence. This tends to make their efforts ineffective and is thus bad for both the individual and the institution.

Now these scenarios are probably more common in education than in industrial practice but all those who have already become enmeshed in any 'Topsy led' innovation will, the writer is sure, recognise the symptoms; it is, of course, far easier to recognise the symptoms than cure the complaint.

Nevertheless, it is suggested that, if the development of learning centres is considered to be important, even those already involved need to pause and review their position while those just beginning should think before they plunge! We need to ask ourselves just *what* we want to do, *why* we want to do it, and *how* best we can do it, in staffing terms, both economically and instructionally.

Now the *how* and the *what* should depend very much on exactly *why* one wants to do something, which is where pragmatism of the sort mentioned above becomes a liability. Tacitly, when open learning is discussed, it is so often assumed that the main switch is that [(individual) + tutor + materials] replaces [(group) + teacher], that the equivalent tuition costs must be overtly comparable and that this determines the amount and type of staff - but does it necessarily do so? Surely this must depend on a combination of the situation, the quality of learning support, the type and pattern of students, and those, in turn, depend on one's reasons for moving into the innovation.

For a 'traditional' distance learning student, the idea of materials plus in-depth tutorials may well be valid and any other staffing considerations are ancillary to this. For centre or workshop students, however, who are probably working largely on site, with supervision and with others around them, the situation is different. They have available what a class student also has but which the home study student almost invariably lacks - what one might term 'casual learning contact' by which is meant the possibility of instantly being able to obtain feedback on a query, to discuss one's problems with those in a similar position or to turn to an alternative source of help and information. The distance learning people effectively acknowledge this need in their recommendations for student self-help groups and similar activities and the reasons are equally valid; so many student problems are really 'low-level', concerned with solving minor difficulties (which only become major difficulties if the student is isolated), with the need for reassurance, with the knowledge that help is readily available if needed. The 'individual tutor' bit then becomes a requirement only when the learner has personal social or emotional problems (which are often connected with isolation) or when specialist knowledge is required and, if the materials are reasonable, that may well be mainly at assessment points.

On the other hand, a continuing physical facility which, ideally, is open whenever its host institution is open (but see chapter 7) has staffing requirements which a distance learning scheme does not. Its actual administration is more complex, for a start, requiring managerial, supervisory and administrative skills in greater quantities while, to achieve the 'casual learning contact' element, it will need to be staffed all or most of the time by someone who can handle the routine queries that any student will have - 'what do I do now', 'I can't grasp this point' - and at the same time organise the place. This may not always be a specialist tutor but there will certainly be need to have such available (the two jobs are not necessarily incompatible). The most vital difference is, perhaps, that you can no longer rely on a small core element and 'buy in' expertise as demand arises; you have to commit resources in advance and encourage business to develop in order to make the scheme viable.

Let us assume, however, that you accept the arguments about financing and up-front commitment discussed in chapter 3 (because if you don't you must try something else). In that case, two immediate questions confront the centre planner:

a) What sort of staff does a particular job need? Although lecturers or training officers get utilised to do it, much of the student processing activity is not academic at all; it consists of booking, general supervision, answering routine queries, etc, all tasks which a competent administrative assistant or library assistant can perform very well and, which is more to the point, more cheaply than academic staff. Thus one should try to avoid using academic staff unnecessarily; every twenty minutes a specialist spends sorting out such problems is twenty minutes of

43

expensive time in which he or she could have been counselling or giving learning advice.

In the same way, one needs to look very carefully at what a centre manager or co-ordinator is tasked to do. How far should he/she be filling in forms and records? Counselling individual students? Sitting in the centre supervising? Or should the job be what its title suggests, co-ordinating those who do perform those tasks? There is a strong temptation for organisations who have just funded a new and expensive post to make its holder do everything because of the perceived cost; that is likely, in the writer's experience, to be false economy in all but the early stages. Appendix 1 provides an analysis of tasks relating to management and co-ordination with suggestions for their allocation.

b)   To take this a little further, are there ways other than the 'personal tutor' concept of providing whatever academic back-up *is* necessary? Well, yes there are and the various subject workshops use them all the time. The basic concept is that of 'covering' specified time periods with appropriate specialist staff who are, as it were, at the beck and call of any students who are using the facility at that time. But horror, shock! How can this be effective, especially in a generalist facility? Surely:

i)   Staff will need to be totally familiar with all the materials or packages being used - just think of the time and the cost (especially that of supplying tutor copies of the packs). Well, not really; one must remember that most if not all of the students are likely to be working at a level of competence well below that of the resident specialist and in practice it has been found that what is a real problem for the student is usually easily resolvable by the 'tutor' even without experience of the actual package the student is working on - if the material is even half-way decent, a quick scan back for a 'page' or two will normally locate the source of difficulty. Indeed, with good individual learning material - and there is an increasing amount available - it is quite possible to do this even in a subject that is not one's own specialism; the writer's Maths, Physics and Biology knowledge increased by leaps and bounds while he was running such a centre! One would not want to make too much of this; there are equally many occasions when deeper knowledge is required but, in the writer's experience, the general thesis holds true. As to the requirement for tutor copies, it is worth remembering that, de facto, a learning centre keeps its material always available for use by its customers so in most cases specialist staff can come in and examine it at will; it may be worth keeping a small library of 'staff copies' but the centre tutor is not normally in the position of having to parallel an individual student throughout his course as the distance tutor does.

ii) Oh? But surely a student needs the continuing attention of the same person who keeps close contact throughout to encourage him and soothe his personal problems? This may certainly be the case for an isolated home study student - and centres may well have a sprinkling of such people among their customers - but again most of a centre's clients are not in that position. If they are internal students or trainees they almost certainly have a mentor in their course tutor or section leader and the continuity of deep-level academic support can usually be achieved by ensuring that relevant specialists are available at the same times each week - either on a 'surgery' basis or as part of their centre-manning duty.

Staffing patterns and densities are, therefore, likely to differ markedly in a centre based scheme from those common to more traditional open learning. So what are the practical implications of these differences?

Implications of Staff Provision and Use
If we have to have 'up-front investment' as the jargoneers like to call it, where are the staff to come from in the first place? Someone (or ones) has to manage and co-ordinate any operation of this type and there are several common ways of providing that function; either personnel (usually a person) are specifically allocated to the job full-time; or one or more persons are formally allocated part of their working time to do it; or (rather too often) an existing senior person simply has the responsibility (though rarely the practical task) added to an existing job-role. Either the first or the third option has been shown to work satisfactorily provided - and only provided - that the appropriate back up is supplied (ie, that a full-time person is of sufficient seniority to carry the load, with the right management links to support him, or that the senior post-holder with responsibility has effective legmen to do the actual work).

What has also been found time and time again is that a part-time

45

appointment to a scheme of this nature is unsatisfactory except where the appointment is directly concerned with the postholder's own line of work and career prospects. In other words a Mathematics section head tasked with developing a Maths workshop has incentive to make it work and the time he puts in will be perceived elsewhere as directly useful. A Geography lecturer, say, given 'time' to develop an open learning provision will tend always to look over his shoulder towards what he sees as his main career prospect and, since many such appointments are relatively junior, is constantly vulnerable to being diverted by his seniors to work which they consider more important. Even a librarian or resource head adding such work to an existing assignment often treats it as an extra which is first to lose out if time presses. The problems of part-time appointments were sharply highlighted by the Open Tech programme where it was found that, although money was allocated to 'free' college staff in delivery systems, in practice the open learning role was usually seen as secondary to other needs; this was particularly so because such staff were often junior and work was very slow to build up so they, apparently, had 'spare time'. It needs to be realised that workload is always slow to build up in an innovation that depends upon external take-up. That is not a reason to recoup the time but an opportunity to allow the person(s) to develop their role.

It is also desirable to distinguish between the institutional co-ordination role and that of a facility manager. The two have frequently been combined in the past, especially in Topsy-led innovations, without giving much thought to conflicts of interest that may arise. For a single facility, the roles may indeed be blurred but, as soon as several facilities are incorporated in a scheme, separation becomes important.

So, to sum up, any manager or co-ordinator needs to be selected as having a real interest in the job and with job conditions that give him a chance of achieving the objectives. To put in a person because his timetable is light (education) or his current post is redundant (industry) is a high risk option!

As regards the staffing time required actually to man a workshop or generalist centre, the same general comments must apply. In order to man a facility properly, and thus make it available to generate student use, the institution has to make an advance staffing commitment, and this is always difficult in an educational context. A bold idea, just now being risked by one or two colleges, is to make such provision a definite college-wide commitment. In this case, the concept is to require each department and section to provide x staff-hours weekly for use in flexible learning - either as specialist tutors or as centre manning, or as a combination of the two (the two roles are not incompatible). That is not too uncommon although it may arouse opposition; the neat extension is that, for their x hours, the section/departments are allowed free use of the centre for y student hours. This at once encourages rethinking of teaching approaches and helps to encourage use in the early stages.

That, for many, must be an ideal and, in this time of demographic decline especially, there must be a temptation for an institution starting any innovation simply to reallocate staff who have spare capacity available. In some cases this can work surprisingly well but it is always likely to lead to problems of motivation and usefulness. In the writer's opinion, backed up by experience, it is just as necessary to pick the 'manning' team carefully as it is to select the leader, at least during the formative period of a centre's development. Once the facility is established as an integral part of the institutional provision the importance is not so great since flexible working can be written into new job descriptions etc and in any case it can be seen as a normal part of the work. In a workshop this is not difficult but in a generalist centre - whether educational or industrial - the change of work mode can cause genuine perturbation both among lecturers and training instructors.

A general, rather than specialist, centre also has some implications for work organisation. In a specialist one, the staff can usually work as a team with much the same interests and expertise and rarely move outside their specialist area of knowledge, while the facility manager is often simply the senior member. A general centre needs a core of generalist staff, able to cope with a variety of subject areas but with periods of selective specialist help; it may also need to have some subject tutors 'on call', so to speak, who may of course have a very easy time at some periods! Hence its staff may be much less focussed, some perhaps only having contact during a few hours a week and thus needing to be structured differently as a team. In this case, the role of the facility manager may be much more of an organising one and he or she may take only a small part in the actual manning.

The writer's preference would be that, for workshops, including those with subject clusters such as business studies, one should concentrate on staffing them with a team of teachers or trainers specialising in that area who really run the facility. Provide administrative back-up in the same way that a laboratory has lab technicians, though if the facility is big enough to have more than one member of staff on duty it will probably pay to ensure one of them is an administrator/receptionist. Generalist rooms, on the other hand, need a different staffing structure: because of the fragmented structure of the tutorial manning, continuity needs to be provided by full-time competent administrative/reception staff with the back-up provided by the tuition staff rather than the other way round.

If one can venture an opinion here, it would seem that the problems encountered by some library or 'learning resource centre' operations which extend into learning centres may occur largely because they do not sufficiently take on board this second element, of regular tuitional staffing; that non involvement may also account for the way that many are perceived as peripheral by the general staff of their institution.

Implications for Management of Learning Centre Staffing

Do management problems in learning centres differ much from those of an educational department, or a training section, one may ask? After all, the general management tasks are very similar: the manager must be able to handle the finances, to organise and be responsible for the physical facilities, to select and control materials, to act as the 'front-man' to liaise with other parts of the institution and to plan strategically. In an industrial context there may well be no other problems and, if an educational centre is seen as a separate part of its institution (as for example a library is), then the situation is similar.

An educational venture, however, rarely develops like that if it is to be successful. The more it integrates into the general work of its institution the more likely it is that staff, even in a subject workshop, will be drawn from a number of departments and sections. Indeed there is a good management argument for doing this where possible in order to involve a number of such departments or sections actively to avoid it being thought of as the preserve of just one part of the organisation and therefore of no consequence to the rest. Hence there will be a particular need for those particular, and often delicate, interpersonal management skills where a balance has to be maintained with staff whose major bosses are elsewhere and effective liaison is vital.

For this reason alone, there seems no alternative to a hierarchical structure, although perhaps a fairly shallow one rather than one with successive levels of responsibility. There needs to be one person in charge, whether reporting to senior institutional management or to a committee of some kind. Colleges tend at present to be appointing such people on Senior or Principal Lecturer grades with direct reporting lines to a Vice-Principal or similar post if they are setting up a scheme from scratch; 'Topsy-led' schemes may well depend on more junior staff carrying out day to day workshop management and reporting to a department head or (historically) being subsumed in a 'Learning Resources Department' which includes facilities thought to be analagous such as the library and media services. It is in no way intended to be derogatory if the writer suggests that such structures should be considered very carefully before being agreed; the problem is not so much that they are perceived as building empires but that their heads inevitably already have main roles to fulfil which, quite naturally, tend to take priority. In the same way, the relationship of an industrial flexible learning centre to its other training activities needs to be considered carefully in a total context. Is the facility an extra? Is it going to be a core part of the training programme? What is its status in the hierarchy?

Further down the line in both education and industry, team management skills will also be vital. This may seem obvious but in practice they are often undervalued. Yet, especially where the staff backgrounds are disparate as they may be in a generalist or multi-workshop operation, the people need to be drawn together as a team, even when they may only have two or three hours weekly allocated to the centre. Unlike conventional classes, students may attend the centre almost randomly and thus obtain help from several members of staff who may each need to know what others have done (see chapter 7 for the recording/

monitoring implications). There is a constant desirability, too, for continuing development feedback between people involved in the centre work. It is worth noting here that the contribution and continuity of a good administrative assistant can be very important indeed. For the institution to consider him or her simply as a secretary/receptionist is to underuse a valuable management resource and it is worth trying to establish any such post on as senior a grade as possible.

Equally, and just as important, man-management skills will be needed because centre-based schemes introduce work modes and work patterns for which few current institutional staff have been trained. Thus, apart from retraining, they may well need help in adapting their own ideas and in adjusting their attitudes to conditions of service under which they may not have worked for some years. Unlike other teaching functions, the concepts of open and flexible learning are not yet firmly enough established for many people to be comfortable with them or to have acquired the necessary tutoring, organisational and monitoring skills in particular.

Lastly, but by no means least, those concerned with managing any centre-based initiative will also need to manage their public relations, both internal and external. As regards the latter, they may well get help from the institution's marketing side but internal publicity and liaison must be their responsibility.

Implications for Staff Training
You may have thought it rather flippant to dismiss 'retraining' in a single phrase just now. How right you were; in an innovation of this type, staff training and professional guidance are very important if only for the man-management reasons cited above. Even enthusiastic volunteers may need guidance in getting away from what is probably the biggest problem of all - our tendency to *teach*. This is not surprising; as professional teachers, we have been almost conditioned into doing this as our basic role but any individualised learning operation (and flexible learning is largely such) will have teaching as only part of its activity. When students are working in the workshop or centre they will be interacting mainly with materials and the staff's role will, or should, change accordingly.

Fortunately there is a great deal of advice available on the different needs of tutoring and teaching, and a selection of the most useful will be found at the end of this section; its only problem for us is that most of it was aimed at distance/open learning schemes and is predicated on the ideal of a personal tutor for each student. Suffice to say here that it does address that major problem which is the teaching urge. As an example, it is common for a student to take a difficulty to the member of staff on duty. What the staff member should do is guide the student over that difficulty and then let him or her carry on; what often happens is that he cannot resist explaining, not just the difficulty but the whole surrounding area of learning which the material is (hopefully) illuminating already.

Staff training and guidance are also needed to counteract what, in another context, the writer has called the Disciple Effect. By this is meant the degradation, in the technical sense, of ideas and designs as they are passed on in succession, further and further away from their original source. When linked with the trite but true saying that 'all systems decay' this is something that needs constant checking. Take as an example an enthusiastic workshop team who make a great effort and produce a complete worksheet scheme for an area of the curriculum; it works well for them and they allow it to be exported to another institution. Now that institution, having had contact with the originators, can use it adequately at first but then staff appear who were not privy to its introduction and by the time they pass it on to the next team the original zest has gone; it is just a set of increasingly dog-eared sheets whose original rationale is often no longer fully comprehended.

This may not happen to the same extent with published materials perhaps because they have been designed with that in mind, but they do have problems of their own; they can get out of date, like textbooks and, because they may be expensive and regarded like library books, are frequently not checked sufficiently often.

In either case the moral is that, just as a teacher needs to refurbish his professional knowledge from time to time, so in a workshop or centre the materials have to be managed and the staff trained to use and develop them intelligently.

Useful References

Davies, I K, *Management of Learning*, McGraw Hill, 1971. This is still the best general introduction to managing learning as opposed to teaching although it is not specifically dealing with learning centres or workshops.

Lewis, R, *How to Tutor and Support Learners* (Open Learning Guide 3), CET, 1984.

Lewis, R, *How to Tutor in an Open Learning Scheme*, CET, 1981. Two useful practical guides; although biased to distance learning they address most of the issues staff will encounter in any flexible learning situation.

Stone, C, *Training Course in Tutoring Open Learning Schemes*, SCOTTSU, 1985. An open learning package on how to tutor.

5. THE PHYSICAL SET-UP: ACCOMMODATION AND LAYOUTS

'In Xanadu did Khubla Khan
A stately pleasure dome decree
Where Alph the sacred river ran
Through caverns measureless to man'
- Samuel Taylor Coleridge

One doesn't know much about Alph (possibly a garrulous caretaker?) and the measureless caverns may well refer to a college Engineering Department, but otherwise Taylor Coleridge obviously had a clear idea of what he wanted from a learning facility in physical terms. Do we?

However you go about setting up a learning centre, and whatever your philosophy, you are going to need a physical set-up somewhere and this needs to be considered under four headings. This aspect *is* important because all too often, like Topsy, it 'just grows': someone starts a workshop in a room that just happens to be empty, even though it is tucked away somewhere in the scruffy parts of an establishment - or is empty just for that reason; an 'open learning office' is sited because that is where the initiator is working and the original layout simply goes along with furniture, etc already in existence. The initial result is not perceived as a problem but if flexible learning does develop as an institutional initiative then such haphazard beginnings can be very restrictive. The results vary, from a single room seating twenty or so (because it was a classroom), through several rooms scattered throughout the establishment because that was how workshops grew up, to a converted hall with a capacity of a hundred or more. All tend to be results of historical accident and only now are a few firms and educational institutions thinking of putting all their facilities together as both a geographical and organisational whole. Yet the complications of getting the planning wrong can be horrendous.

We would suggest that, if at all possible, any physical facilities need to be considered in conjunction with each other from the start and with regard to their overall size, siting and appearance. Indeed appearance is becoming quite vital as overall standards in public places, shops, etc become higher; the common-user spaces in both educational and training institutions tend to get hard wear and look as though they do but many private trainers - and some colleges - have realised that volunteer learners now expect something better. There is, or should be, almost a social element in learning and, if the cameraderie of a homogeneous group is not present, a relaxing atmosphere, conducive to making individual contacts, needs to take its place. Let us look first, then, at accommodation.

It may be banal but it is true to say that the type and quantity of accommodation should depend on what facilities are going to be required. The ideal for an institution-wide operation has to be a suite of rooms as a central base. This is not for prestige reasons, though it is a good marketing ploy, but because of the operational flexibility and efficiency it bestows; security is easier to control, staffing can be deployed more efficiently, spaces can be used more flexibly to cope with student flows. This is particularly so if a multirole facility is envisaged. Workshops can be self-contained though they, too, benefit by being able to spill over into other space at peak periods and assimilation within general flexible learning provision will tend to diminish 'special interest' exclusiveness which may otherwise develop.

Of the various flexible approaches, distance learning is often perceived as the simplest in terms of physical provision, making very few demands. The student can use existing facilities such as libraries (true) and tutorials, counselling, etc can be done in existing staff offices (not quite so true). Yes, it can work like that but have you considered:

a) The public relations effect of prospective students having to find an, often rather grotty, room in the back-ends of a building.

b) The operational inefficiency of having to conduct interviews and tutoring sessions, possibly with other people in a shared staff room.

In the writer's opinion, therefore, the minimum requirement, even for pre-packaged distance learning, is a bright, welcoming office somewhere near reception, dedicated to student interviewing and preferably adjacent to a comfortable space where materials and notices can be displayed and where students can work. Some form of seminar facilities will be needed at times as well and home study students do need a focal area in which they can meet and relax. Working largely on your own is, for most people, not the wonderful experience the glossy TV advertisements portray. People need support and to be able to talk with others in a similar situation.

The next most simple provision, at least in accommodation terms, is probably the single subject workshop. This basically needs a suitably equipped and fairly large room for student use, preferably with a small partitioned space nearby for tutorial and other advice sessions with individuals or small groups. So long as the spaces can be dedicated to workshop use, organisation is not difficult. Alas, all too often, the initiative has to start as a small, rather peripheral activity - perhaps on just two or three sessions a week - using a room that is, at other times, employed as a normal classroom. While it cannot always be avoided, organisers should realise that such a situation is very unfavourable to further development. It is very restrictive when trying to plan student programmes, the furniture, being dual purpose, is often not well adapted for individual use and it becomes very difficult to have materials readily available or displayed.

It is suggested, therefore, that any institution seriously considering setting up such workshops should try to give them dedicated accommodation from the start. There may be uncomfortable gaps in usage to start with but, in the writer's experience, Parkinson's Law applies; if the materials, etc are attractive, occupation expands to fill the time available even with a single subject. Indeed it is quite common for such workshops to become fully loaded even when covering only one subject area for part of the institution. If that happens there will naturally be a demand for more accommodation but it is probably sensible to examine carefully what the existing usage is, rather than just trying to expand automatically. In particular, look to see whether you are in danger of doing things that could, just as well, be carried out in a normal classroom - for example are complete groups coming in just to work through the same few worksheets? If so, would it not be more sensible to organise matters so that those worksheets can be exported to the normal class working space which could otherwise be empty? True, it may be argued that the motivating factor of coming into a workshop is important but that has to be set against the disadvantages for other students. In any case it can reasonably be argued that a workshop is a way of working rather than a place and that, so long as the materials and advice are properly organised, some aspects - and these include group work - can be successful anywhere. Do remember that large-group based and individual operations do not sit comfortably together; one has only to look at the distraction in most college libraries when a group is carrying out a 'library period' to see that. The main criterion for using the special accommodation, surely, must be whether you have people carrying out a wide range of learning tasks that require use of the full facilities.

The next arrangement to consider, the generalised learning room or learning centre, may at first sight be thought of just as a variant of a workshop, at least so far as accommodation is concerned. Since the intention behind any such facility is to provide a wide range of individual learning schemes, most of which will be heavily materials-based, it is frequently argued that special accommodation is not really necessary; its natural place is as part of an extended institutional library and, in some institutions, that is where it is. At the risk of offending his librarian friends, the writer would say that this course of action has its dangers; the additional space, which usually has to be carved out of existing library territory, is often cramped, sometimes has to be dual use and is, in any case, inhibited by the common perceptions of a library's function. It is commonly accepted that this is to provide access to information; what the client does with that information once located is not normally the concern of the library staff though they may well help in its selection.

On the other hand a learning centre, whether macro or microcosmic, is basically there actively to promote learning and to help a student through the learning process. It therefore requires a different ethos, organisation and staffing pattern which, in turn, has implications for the accommodation. This may certainly, with advantage, be situated adjacent to library facilities and may even, for purposes of security and ambience, be entered from them, but it needs to be a dedicated room or rooms specifically organised for its purpose. Ironically, because such a facility is specifically for individuals or small groups and usually an 'extra', this may well mean in the early days that it will be beautiful but underused; nonetheless, as with a workshop, it is not wise to try to fill its time up with overflow classes. In doing so the essential flexibility will be lost and this becomes a vicious circle.

There is a problem of what we have referred to as the 'macro' concept of a learning centre - the provision of a structure or organisation for co-ordinating the institution's non-class based approaches. If the historical and geographical constraints dictate it, this may well physically have to consist of a number of separated learning spaces (libraries, workshops, learning and tutorial rooms, practical facilities) co-ordinated from a central office. In such a case all the above comments apply, overlaid with the need for the co-ordinating function to have accurate and updated information about usage, space availability, etc and also for intercommunication to take place. At the very least it will be desirable for all points to be on the internal telephone network.

Ideally, however, it is probably desirable for the various facilities all to be together under one roof and adjacent to each other. The ease of client access, the operational convenience and the flexibility of being able to overflow between spaces must outweigh any disadvantages. The occasionally voiced criticism that, especially on a scattered site, workshops should be sited near major users is valid only if the major user is a single section or department - and in that case the major criterion of cross-institutional value is unlikely to be realised.

Equally, if it is physically possible, it is desirable to site at least the reception/display facilities, and preferably the whole facility, as close as possible to the main centre of institutional life and as obviously easy of access as possible.

In a training department, it is no bad thing if both staff and clients - whether trainees or other divisions of the firm - actually enter the department either through or just by an active learning facility; it may well give them cause to think! In an educational institution exposure to the clientele, both actual and potential, can only be advantageous if it is attractive to look at and demonstrates ease of access; it is a good marketing ploy in both instances.

Lastly, but by no means least, there are many advantages to be gained by providing an attractive atmosphere as we have already mentioned. Adults in particular are unlikely to return to school-like classrooms by choice; if they do not overtly grumble, either in industrial or educational circumstances, it is, we suggest, probably because they are not normally offered anything better. If they come voluntarily and you want to encourage them as individuals to use your physical plant, then some carpeting, pleasant lighting, functional but neat furniture and, preferably, a space where they can sit with others and relax socially will cost something in the short term but may equally return considerable benefits eventually; just why we should so often be expected to learn in bleak and uninviting conditions is hard to understand except in terms of perceived economic expediency.

Implications for Accommodation
The implications, bluntly, are that purpose-designed or adapted accommodation dedicated to flexible learning must be largely superior to multi-use spaces. In terms of user satisfaction, it will undoubtedly pay:

a) To site the facilities together and in an easily accessible and well-signposted position; the latter is especially important if much external use is envisaged.

b) To provide a high standard of furnishing and equipment so that it is a pleasure to work in the facility. This does have the additional implication that such standards need to be maintained.

c) To provide a range of physical facilities including: communal work spaces for individual learning; small rooms/partitioned spaces for interviews and seminars; a comfortable social area for students to relax in and obtain the 'casual learning contact' that is so important.

Unless there are social facilities near at hand, the social area is also important if a quiet study atmosphere is to prevail in the actual work spaces, especially in a general purpose facility where the range of students may be diverse. Individual work has to depend mainly on self-discipline and it is vital that learner concentration is not disturbed by those who feel the need to take a break.

Implications for Layouts
Taking all the foregoing into account, are there any useful recommendations that one can make as to layouts for a learning room or workshop
of any kind? The answer, fortunately, is yes. There is now a wide range
of experience ranging from small library resource centres to lavish all-
purpose areas such as that at the former Dundee College of Education
although, surprisingly, there appears to be little actually published
about the physical design of actual learning facilities. Any detail design
must obviously depend on the size and shape of the room(s) involved
and on the exact purpose of the facility but there are general parameters
that are common to all.

Perhaps the most important thing to remember is that any such facility
is likely to be used mainly by individuals rather than groups and that this
need should not be compromised - classrooms in which the desks are
hastily regrouped when a 'workshop period' comes round may
occasionally be expedient but are not conducive either to efficiency or
relaxed learning. Overall the ambience of any learning room needs to be
pleasant, the spaces need to be easily monitored and secure, the lighting
needs to be good and adapted to the needs of individuals rather than
consisting just of serried ranks of flourescent tubes marching inflexibly
across the ceiling. Those requirements in themselves must have some
constraints on design and the requirements of individual workstations
impose others.

As to the requirements of individual workstations, fashions appear to be
changing - and probably for the better as a whole. In the 1970s, in the
(premature) white heat of the technological revolution, great emphasis
was placed on the individual carrel or study booth, no doubt based on
the seclusion needs of serious academic scholars. Most carrels were
designed almost to enclose the student, with high backs and side screens
stretching up to or past the seating line. There was also a strong tendency
to assume that at least a proportion of them required built-in media
devices and that, ideally, these should be fed from a central point rather
on the language laboratory principle.

Now, up to a point, this is an excellent idea *provided the technology works*
but, in the more parsimonious 1980s, it has been recognised that it is

distinctly wasteful of expensive resources, particularly in educational establishments. It may still be fine for a commercial or in-company high-tech centre where students are either paying their way or are being trained on a fairly restricted range of programmes but for a general purpose educational facility it seems needlessly elaborate and the law of diminishing returns applies. Carrels themselves are still popular as a basic workstation module and, to be fair, five years ago the writer would have been recommending them wholeheartedly. Now, with the prospect of less selective usage by a greater range of possibly less motivated students, it may be that the needs of security and student monitoring are greater than those of individual seclusion.

Indeed from observation there is little evidence that the blinkered world of a full carrel has great advantages; like a horse in a constraining stall, learners from time to time feel impelled to push back their chairs or peer across the partitions out of curiosity or the need for company. They certainly appear, as a generalisation, not to be unduly worried by seeing other people working alongside them so long as belongings do not wander into 'their' space. The indications are that backscreens are more important, both to provide a screen immediately ahead and as a support for shelving, etc. There is something, therefore, to be said for fairly large furniture modules of long deep tables (deep because of the need to write as well as to use equipment) with fairly low backscreens on which can be mounted bookracks and electric power outlets - rather like modernised laboratory benches, which is, indeed, not a bad analogy to have in mind. Free-standing equipment can then be installed with no awkward cable runs and the whole ensemble is both easy to use, to monitor and to keep clean.

The major exception to this 'open plan' layout may need to be where intrusive noise is involved. In the writer's experience not too much needs to be made of low level mechnical noise (keyboarding, etc) unless it becomes obtrusive. Learners, once concentrating, appear generally able to filter it out but voices or loud noises such as music or conventional typing may need to be acoustically screened in some way. It is accepted that these are personal observations and not always to everyone else's taste; those with different views can find detailed information regarding carrel design, etc in the references at the back of this chapter. What everyone does seem agreed on is that a comfortable working chair is needed for each learner, a well designed typing chair on casters being as good as any, and that lighting, preferably without glare, needs to be sited to illuminate the working space with the minimum of shadow.

General layouts, as opposed to individual ones, must depend on the type and shape of the accommodation and on the proposed use. A workshop, where students may be frequently wanting to change assignments or worksheets and so move about, will have different requirements from a centre in which most learners are working on lengthy packages; a purely internal facility can get away without the display arrangements that may be desirable in a room setting out to entice and inform the general public. In both, however, one major determinant is that, as in public transport, passenger flow should be paramount; movement to, from and around the facility should be so planned as not unduly to disturb those already working.

Lastly, although in theory it should not be necessary, the layout should allow for maximum security. Not only media devices but also packages can be very costly these days and many components of them are what the police euphemistically describe as 'attractive'; a device or package that is incomplete is as useless as if it had been taken entirely. It is, therefore, desirable that the room(s) be laid out so that it can be visually supervised from a single point. Increasingly, materials in particular are being coded by their users to fit in with electronic surveillance systems and this is a very sensible idea; it is one good argument for working closely with the institution's library which is likely to have experience in such systems and also to have the physical scanning devices already installed.

Useful References
As noted, there is little useful information in print on this aspect of learning facility design but the following do contain some useful ideas; most, however, are school-biased.

Atherton, B, *Adapting Spaces for Resource-Based Learning* (Guidelines 8), CET, 1980.

Davies, W J K, *Alternatives to Class Teaching in Schools and Colleges* (Guidelines 9), CET, 1980.

Walton, J (ed), *Resources and Resource Centres*, Ward Lock, 1975.

6. LEARNING CENTRE MATERIALS AND MEDIA

Does your chewing gum lose its flavour on the bedpost overnight?
                                    - '60s pop song

Or, more pertinently, do your learning packages and equipment moulder away in cupboards all covered in dust? Because if they do it is a sure sign that your learning facility has not been well thought through. As mentioned in chapter 1, any open or flexible learning approach is, by definition, based on the widespread use of resource materials which are intended to take over at least some of the teaching and learning function; only by offloading some of this can any individualised or learner centred provision work economically, so they ought to be in constant use.

That is generally accepted; far less so is what sorts of materials should be provided and how they should be used: should they be bought in or should they be home-grown? And how elaborate should they be? Indeed the odd thing is that, at least up to now, there has been an almost complete split in practice between those institutions, or sections of them, which entered flexible learning through what we have called 'traditional OL' - flexistudy, delivery of the Open Tech programme, more recently the Open College - and those which came in by 'supported self-study' or the learner-centred requirements of accrediting bodies such as BTEC and City & Guilds. The former group tends to assume that the way ahead is to use existing packages which they see themselves as buying and selling on, with 'value-added' support; the latter feel that they know best what is needed and how to provide it. The 'not invented here' syndrome is still very strong in British education although to a lesser extent in industrial training because that tends to cost out the consequences of its decisions.

It is, of course, far too sweeping to say that the twain never meet; in the more enlightened places they do, to excellent effect. Nonetheless there are widespread adversarial perceptions which get disseminated and any institution or company initiating a flexible learning policy needs to be able both to design and produce, and to use existing materials as economically and effectively as possible. It may, therefore, be worth looking at the advantages and problems of each approach.

The 'homebrew' approach has many perceived advantages. To start with, the materials can be built exactly to fit the learning requirements and the particular approach that is adopted. They can take many and varied forms, as against the pre-structured nature of ready-made packages; worksheets, assignments, proper self-study units can all be incorporated within the same study programme and their inherent flexibility allows rapid changes to be made. In practice, most such materials are guideline or assignment based because of the effort involved and they require a fair amount of support but this can certainly be seen as an advantage. There is, hence, plenty of advice available on how to write or adapt such materials and the approach is widely encouraged if for no other reason than that we all feel better with something we have created.

Those are some of the advantages but their proponents rarely stress the downsides. These are that the cost is often not particularly cheap even if the efforts involved in writing are effectively discounted by enthusiasm; it is not unknown for a department to recoil in horror on finding the bill for simple reprographics to equip one Maths workshop has reached over £2,000 - and that is for consumable materials. If the true costs to the institution in staff time, material and reprographics, trials and revisions are worked out - not to mention the opportunity costs involved - then it often means that very serious consideration is needed before embarking on a project of any size. There is also the matter of quality. No-one would claim that commercial materials are necessarily of high quality just because they are published but many homegrown ones work only with a dangerously high level of support in economic terms. That may be acceptable so long as their initiators are around but the acid test is whether they will still work satisfactorily after their creators have gone. If they do not, then investment ends up as piles of paper gathering dust.

Equally, the advantages of pre-prepared packages are often hymned by the high-pressure salesforces of commercial publishers. They have been 'carefully designed and tried out' (often true); they can be made much more attractive to the student; many are 'designed and approved for learning leading to external accreditation' (no-one points out that the institution has to negotiate this with the relevant body); most are 'basically modular' (but were not necessarily planned with that in mind).

Again their advocates tend to forget the disadvantages as seen by many of their potential clients; they were not invented here and so are dubious - and it is very easy to pick holes in someone else's work although in most cases the minor criticisms do not affect a package's total validity. The occasional glaringly bad product, usually though not always from small concerns that are just enthusiasts writ large, tends to reinforce this criticism. Then the unit cost is perceived as very high which it often is. It must be said that, so far, producers have not helped themselves here. In being led to assume that industry was the main customer and that industry does not mind paying high prices for 'one-shot' material, they tended deliberately to design packs so that they are not easily reusable. One pack, one student has been the slogan which might have worked had the package unit cost been relatively low. Fortunately the more enlightened publishers are now producing reusable packs with consumable workbooks, etc where initial cost is a serious factor, so that this criticism is beginning to lose its force.

The other main perceived disadvantage of ready-made packages, particularly the high-tech ones, is that it is not easy to 'unwrap' them in order to see what is inside and how good they are - and this is important if the institution's credibility depends upon customer satisfaction. There is currently no satisfactory answer to this problem. One can only hope both that producers improve their documentation and that more objective reviews become widely available.

The general perception of all this, however, has been that published packages are expensive and usable mainly as peripheral extras for home study while homegrown materials are something any institution can undertake. As a consequence, a good deal has been written about how to write and adapt materials and (implicitly) on how to manage them in a scheme; far less has been written on how to *use* existing materials in anything other than a 'traditional OL' way. Yet percept-ions of the essential costing of both methods may well be based on fallacies:

a) The grow-your-own philosophy has considerably underplayed the true costs to an institution of providing an enduring scheme; they can certainly be hidden if material is enthusiast generated *but* a responsible institution will need to ensure that such materials are usable by others so that when its initiators leave, the whole process does not have to start again. That means a proper design, production, trial, revision process and that, in turn, means a real cost in any terms; a costed figure of 20 man-hours per student work-hour for preparation alone has often been quoted and is not unreasonable.

b) The 'ready-use' advocates have not necessarily done themselves a service by insisting on the buy and sell-on philosophy. This has tended both to marginalise the general market and also discourage internal use, because the perceived unit cost is very high. One can understand the short-term urge of suppliers for repeat business but if a package can be reused a number of times (see later) then its true cost comes down towards the perceived expense of method (a). It might be a different market place in which publishers base their run on selling a large number initially plus either a licence or additional workbooks (rather as some books depend on library purchases for their print run) but the result for producers might be surprisingly similar while increasing educational take-up.

That, however, is something of a digression. The interesting point is that, properly managed, the adjusted costs are probably about equal for either approach. They therefore give institutions a chance in practice to mix and match rather than use either approach exclusively - provided the philosophy is right.

'So what?' do I hear you ask? All this 'on the one hand... and on the other hand. . .' is all very well but how does it help to make decisions? The author would argue that innovation is always bedevilled by preconceptions and unpremeditated enthusiasms and second-stage innovation (which this has now become) is even more prone to those problems; it certainly behoves institutional management to consider the background carefully before coming to a decision as to how to proceed.

That having been said, what is the best way to organise and provide materials for use in a flexible learning scheme? There used to be a useful little adage in industrial training that ran something like this:

'First of all try to simplify the task so that as much as possible can be done without training (or identify those parts that don't need it: accreditation of pre-acquired learning is probably the educational equivalent!). Then see what you can solve by providing job-aids and guidance of various kinds; train for the residue but regard this more as a last resort than an inevitable process.'

In educational resource terms, the equivalent procedure might be:

a)   Use what is available where it is suitable.

b)   If there is only partly suitable material, adapt it or provide extra guidance where possible.

c)   Write new material only if you cannot avoid it (and then produce in assignment form if possible, rather than full self-study packs).

It is, therefore, sensible for anyone setting up flexible learning facilities to know just what is available - and there is a wide and increasing range of ready-made materials; to have some philosophy for deciding on the quality of available materials and to have thought of the total range of uses to which they may be put. Users also need to consider whether they necessarily need to sell materials on or whether the materials are reusable and so could be employed for on-site work, or as a lending (renting?) library, thus reducing the package element in any student cost (see chapter 2).

With regard to what is available, there are plenty of published lists and sources - the reading list at the end of this chapter gives some guidance. That is comparatively easy! Evaluation is more difficult because, just as with textbooks, there are only ephemeral reviews available. However, if you are considering existing materials, do at least look for the following features: does the documentation describe clearly what the package sets out to achieve (its objectives) and how it works; does it quantify how much support is needed; if costly, does the package contain reusable and consumable elements - workbooks provided, for instance; is any consumable element structured to be useful to the student as a continuing work of reference, or can you add to or adapt materials to make this so?

Does it contain internal assessment devices? In Appendix 2 is a useful checklist to help you carry out this operation.

To find out if the material is acceptable to students is much harder since one person's meat is another one's poison. Remember only that it is unlikely to have been written for *you*; in most cases the target audience may be less advanced in learning (but may conversely know things about the subject you do not) or vice versa. It is difficult to judge and the writer can remember many a time wanting to reject packages which turned out to work very successfully with those for whom they were intended.

Another problem, which relates mainly to the use of published materials, is that, for economy reasons, a complete course is often bound up in one volume or integrated package on the assumption that a student will work right through it. With the increasing interest in modularisation and training for specific tasks, this can be a hindrance as you find suitable material of which only a section is needed - a problem that becomes even more irritating when two or more students could work on different sections if only they were not bound together! With the increasing duplication of material provision in popular areas (eg office studies) it is therefore worthwhile using the inherent flexibility of a package as one of your criteria for choosing it, or at least seeing if you can physically split up the artefact.

If, on the other hand, it is suggested that an institution produces its own materials, first ask why it needs to do such a thing and exactly what does it want to do? Who are the materials for - especially the size of the audience - and how is it intended to organise their use? If you can define these factors early on, then you can get a good idea of the real costs and so see if the approach is a realistic one. The vital fact to remember is that the correlation between materials quality and the amount of support has been shown over and over again to be valid. The more imperfect (even if cheaper) the materials, the greater the cost of support mechanisms if they are to be effective; the better (not necessarily more expensive) the materials, the lower support costs should be. In a workshop or centre situation, with helpful staff around, you may be able to get away with less polished material than for distance learning, though you need to check that it is comprehensible to others than those who wrote it. Conversely material written for distance learning will usually work well in a workshop because of the extra care that had to go into the material's design to enable it to work with little support.

Perhaps the most unrecognised problem bedevilling the development of open and flexible learning centres, however, is the question of how best to use the available materials, from whatever source. Let us have a look at various options:

a) Use on-site, like a reference library.

b) Sell-on and forget.

c) Use as 'throw-away' items - ie issued free or at little cost and designed to be consumable - worksheets are an example.

d) Loan or rent, with intent to recoup and recycle.

All these have been used on occasions, though only (b) and (c) have found widespread favour. Those running workshops have tended to go for (c), though sometimes with an admixture of (a) leading to very grubby and dog-eared material after a while; open learners, with their propensity for home learning, have tended to go for (b). Do notice we said 'tended'; there are of course schemes which show the converse but very few genuine learning operations have in the past adopted (d) and fewer still have tried to use all the options. The writer suggests that institutions setting up flexible learning facilities should deliberately consider a 'mix and match' policy to serve different needs rather than just settle on one option. The main basis could well be to encourage people to work on site if the material is hard wearing and expensive. There is a good deal to be said for having reusable materials which students come in to use. Even allowing for wear and tear, the attributable cost per student is minimised, the social and 'casual learning' aspects of group education and training are maintained and the physical plant of the institution is utilised - which it is not in home learning schemes.

On the other hand, some students may need or want to take packages away. In such cases material can either be 'throw-away' or more permanent items can be loaned against a deposit or rented, thus cutting the cost to a student while amortising the cost of the package over several issues. Lastly, there will always be home study students who will feel the need for a pack of their own and are prepared to pay, in which case 'sell-on' is a viable option. The writer would only submit that it need not be thought of as the main one.

Implications of Media Choice

So far we have been talking of materials as though the media in which they are presented is unimportant. It is true that, even at the time of writing, the great majority of packages, and almost all home-produced materials, are print based and this may well stay that way for the forseeable future; much learning and training does not actually require the elaborate mediated packages that media enthusiasts and suppliers like to provide. There are, however, plenty of occasions when a particular medium is appropriate - for example CBT is a sensible method of teaching computer applications; moving pictures require the use of video. The danger lies between the extremes of buying a lot of expensive equipment and then trying to find material to justify the purchase, and hoping to install appropriate media devices only when a need arises. At the risk of appearing too basic, it may be worth recapping on the main complex media that find their way into flexible learning schemes:

Video: this is simply a videocassette recorder which can be used to record off-air or replay prerecorded programmes via a television set. In open learning applications it is normally used for the latter purpose, many learning packages having a videocassette element. Sometimes these are essential, sometimes simply an optional extra. There is a tendency, which those planning centres should guard against, to regard any video as being suitable for self-study.

Microcomputer: the microcomputer, which is self-explanatory, is in use in flexible learning both as an instrument for training in control functions (eg robotics) and as a means of interfacing between a learning programme and the student. Computer Based Training (CBT), which uses the micro itself to teach applications, is becoming popular in industry and an increasing number of packages utilise this method; many others include a computer disc (the old cassette has, thankfully, almost disappeared) to present simulations or complex material to work through. The major problem is that what works on one machine may not do so on another and that even discs come in different sizes.

Interactive video: basically a combination of the two technologies above, normally using a microcomputer to select video images off a pre-recorded, random-access source. Typically this is a proprietary read-only videodisc rather than a tape (because of speed of access). The intention behind the technology is to combine computing power with the visual and audio quality obtainable from video and thus provide a very flexible device. Its main problem at present is that the technology is ahead of the producers and much so-called interactive video material does not need the technology at all.

A general purpose workshop needs a selection of such items - microcomputers, video sets, even cassette tape recorders but unless it is specifically high tech it needs small numbers of each rather than a huge battery. However well designed, videos, microcomputers and the like take up space and space is usually at a premium. Of course, if the workshop application is specifically high tech or the institution already has a computer workshop with spare capacity, such restrictions do not apply. The best advice the writer can give is to examine carefully the range of mediated materials you want and see what they run on. For example, at the time of writing, most of the usable software that is of value in skills training runs on IBM PCs or fully compatible IBM clones - and some require upgraded software. Partly compatible machines, or those designed for educational use are not of much value unless the individualised packages peculiar to them are required. Likewise there is always a media device at the forefront of technology; currently it is interactive video which would seem to have great potential but comparatively little really useful material.

Implications for Materials Use *(for problems of acquisition and administration, see chapter 7)*
The implications for centre and workshop managers can largely be reduced to a series of aide memoires, viz:

71

a) Try to establish what the centre use pattern is likely to be. You may wish to use the facility for groups, in which case there is a need to acquire multiple copies, although not necessarily one per student since there is no reason why all students should work on the same thing at once. On the other hand, the centre may be concerned mainly with individuals, in which case a wide variety of single copies is desirable but several copies of the more popular items may be needed.

b) These comments assume that most of the work will be done on-site, as in a reference library, because that is undoubtedly the most cost-effective way of using packages. If, however, students wish or need to take materials away, the centre has to set up arrangements for selling, renting or loaning packages. In this context especially, it needs to recognise that any formalised material starts to become out of date as soon as it is published and the stock will need to be kept under constant review both for physical condition and for relevance.

c) Always try to find out what is already available before constructing your own material and try, at least, to assess whether it has the features that are likely to aid success; but don't forget that what you like may appear unsuitable to students and vice versa. If you cannot find suitable packages, consider adapting or modifying before you start writing from scratch.

d) Certainly use complex media where appropriate but don't get ensnared by it because it looks attractive.

e) Remember that all materials start becoming obsolete as soon as they are produced and while you can easily update teaching notes, pre-structured materials are more difficult.

f) Don't get blinkered.

Useful References
Reference sources
Adapting Training Materials for Open Learning and *Writing Open Learning Materials*, both SCOTTSU, 1985. Two open learning courses on materials production.

Lewis, R and Paine, N, *How to Find and Adapt Materials and Select Media* (Open Learning Guide 8), CET, 1986. A useful general guide to getting on with existing materials.

Romiszowski, A J, *Selection and Use of Instructional Media*, Kogan Page, 1974. A very detailed study of instructional media and their effects. Although outdated in relation to the latest technology, it is excellent for material producers.

Organisations
National Council for Educational Technology, 3 Devonshire Street, London W1N 2BA (formerly CET). A very useful source of information on microcomputing and all other aspects of educational technology including open and flexible learning.

National Interactive Video Centre, 24-32 Stephenson Way, London NW1 2HD. Currently the best source of information about interactive video developments.

7. LEARNING CENTRE OPERATION AND ADMINISTRATION

'Oh I am the cook and the captain bold,
And the mate of the Nancy Brig,
And the bosun tight, and the midshipmite,
And the crew of the captain's gig'
- W S Gilbert, Bab Ballads

All college vice-principals and most training officers have known this feeling at some time or another. What is not so often remembered is that it might well be also the song of a learning centre manager; he or she, as published job descriptions testify, is often expected to perform a wide variety of roles and often with very little formal training: administration; publicity and marketing; student supervision, monitoring and guidance; internal and external liaison of a proactive type - all need to be covered.

In practice, it may prove sensible to split some of the roles up because otherwise they may be so diverse as to be carried out ineffectively. Nevertheless they are needed because, to be cost effective, a learning facility has to attract clients who come back again and again; to do that it must leave its students with the feeling that they have been successful and well supported and its 'sponsors' - student course leaders or employers, for instance - feeling that they have been well looked after. So what aspects of operation are particularly significant and unique to such facilities?

Probably the first is what one might describe as 'use control'. In the early days, while use builds up, it may not seem important to have elaborate administration procedures but their presence will become necessary all too soon if it succeeds. We need therefore, when setting up a centre or wokshop, to consider not just its initial needs but how usage is likely to develop. We must ask how the centre or workshop is likely to be used. By groups replacing timetabled classes at fixed times? By internal individual students or groups at more or less fixed times for assignment work? As planned self-study by internal students? By external students on a drop in basis? By supporting students in their workplace (which

75

may be a function especially of company centres)? Or by combinations of these? Clearly this has implications for manning because homogeneous groups are different from a constantly fluctuating collection of individuals working on widely different subjects and a use pattern that requires individual students to be 'in-filled' among existing users is different from one where groups are an exception and the individual priorities are paramount. Likewise, it has implications for the periods of opening, for student monitoring procedures and for general liaison and marketing.

As regards opening periods, it is common for educational workshops especially to be open, at least initially, only for limited periods during the week and often as uneasy occupants of a space that is used for class groups at other times. The arguments are that space is always short, that staff can only be allocated when they can be redeployed from conventional teaching and that to have a room standing idle is wasteful. No-one would deny that there is a force to such arguments and, where the innovation is enthusiast generated, this situation may be necessary in the short term. Where an institution is intending deliberately to set up any such facility on a wider basis, however, the writer suggests that it should think long and carefully before allowing such a situation to occur; as has been shown with traditional open learning, if you advertise a need and then cannot meet it, the opportunity tends to be lost for good.

What applies to subject workshops must be even more important with a generalist centre, especially in an educational establishment. Here it is much more likely that usage will be wide and varied; there is even an increasing question as to whether clients will be satisfied with normal educational patterns of use. Will they, for instance, require at least some opening times in college vacations (after all, libraries are normally open for most of these). The advocated ideal is, of course, 9.00 am to 9.00 pm (or thereabouts) every working day but in practice extent of service initially often has to be balanced against cost. Unless there is a guaranteed clientele - for example a group whose work has been individualised - the important thing is to ensure that the facility is initially available for at least part of every day together with at least some evening sessions and to ensure a reasonable distribution of specialist staff help (see chapter 4), with the intention of building up availability as use develops.

One therefore has the extremes of limited use, mainly for groups, with the premises otherwise unavailable, and a totally available facility. The further one gets towards the latter, the more vital the actual 'use control' factors such as booking and student recording become. Space may be limited, specific items of equipment or packages even more so, so all the staff need to know some time ahead just what is free; students may wish to reserve, or even borrow (rent?), packages so some form of loan system will be needed. Not only staff but management may need to know how the facility is developing and what its patterns of use are. It is surprising how many individual students can be processed during a working week without a reasonable-sized room looking anything like full, except at peak periods; this may make it difficult sometimes to convince management that the scheme is working unless hard statistical evidence is available! These items are discussed in detail below under 'practical implications' but are raised here because they affect the other aspects of operation.

Of these, the one most closely related to use control is that of monitoring students' progress (as opposed to their physical presence). This again is a task peculiar to individualised work if undertaken in depth and its intensity depends on the answer to one question: to what extent is the centre expected to monitor and guide directly its clients' programme? A library or learning resource centre of traditional type, for example, normally just provides facilities and supervision, leaving the actual progress control to others such as course tutors. A learning centre or workshop, on the other hand, will probably need to take at least some responsibility for what it does. The extent will differ between the assignment-oriented or supported self-study scheme where students are sent by tutors to do something specified externally and then to report back for guidance, and the centre or workshop-based approach where guidance and at least some degree of assessment is likely to be built in (this is especially so in the situation where a client is likely to come of his own volition and use the centre as his main learning base). For this, in particular, some form of student record and monitoring system is essential, especially if the student comes at several times when different staff are on duty. It may also be required to support evidence of progress towards a qualification or competence in a particular learning task.

The monitoring and guidance of students blends almost imperceptibly into the third aspect of centre operation, that of how to integrate its functions into the general life of its institution, whether educational or industrial. As has been mentioned earlier, there is a considerable danger of isolation and neglect unless the centre or workshop is perceived as being a genuine option for students and one that makes a positive contribution to other aspects of the establishment's work. Here, it is suggested, actions speak louder than words. If the facility helps to solve problems, if it can be shown to be effective in learning and, especially in education, if it actually helps to increase a market share, then it is its own best advocate. Nonetheless, its sponsors and management need to accept that, particularly in the early stages, there is an active liaison and marketing job to be done and that is an integral part of operating.

Last but not least, any facility of this nature needs to have established procedures for physical control of its plant and stock. This may appear so obvious as not to be worth mentioning; after all libraries, science labs and training departments as a whole appear to operate without any fuss. What tends to be forgotten is that they operate on procedures already established through years of familiarity; an innovatory operation has to establish them from scratch even if it chooses to adapt existing ideas. To reiterate, therefore, it needs to have formal procedures for controlling its budget, for maintaining and updating its equipment, and for ordering, maintaining and replacing its package stock as necessary. This last, in particular, does present some fresh problems since the stock necessarily turns over fairly quickly, can quickly become out of date and requires some measure of evaluation input to help ensure a high quality. There may also be a need to sell packages or to make short or long term loans, possibly against some form of deposit and/or rental payment, which in turn requires at least some financial procedures. Indeed the facility, or at least the 'macro' centre, may well have a budget of its own which will need to be managed.

Implications for Centre Management
Use control
The easiest system to operate is undoubtedly a subject workshop with a high proportion of class use and it is very tempting to start with this and the barest essentials. Once random individuals are involved, however,

matters quickly become more complex. On the principle of being prepared, the writer suggests that it is sensible from the start to put in a booking and student control system that can cope with such complexity, even if it appears cumbersome for small numbers. Trying to retrieve a backlog is always difficult and an initial comprehensive system has the advantage that one can monitor intensity and patterns of use from the very beginning. Where the organisation incorporates more than one workshop or centre, the physical circumstances will determine if the system can be centralised (economical) or whether separate ones need to be run for each facility.

What sort of system? The basis should be threefold:

1. A booking book or computerised equivalent showing the availability of spaces plus any specialised equipment or single-copy packages for two or three weeks ahead. In this area microdatabase programs such as Dataease or the DBASE series have made maintenance of such a system much easier once set up so are in general to be preferred to a book because of the variables involved (you may need to know, for a given time, if a specified CBT package *and* an appropriate machine are free, for example). A useful optional extra is a wipe-clean wall chart displaying the current day's situation at a glance; this is particularly helpful if 'drop-in' facilities are being provided.

2. An individual student record form which the student can fill in, thus relieving some pressure on staff. At the least this needs to show the student's name - and contact if appropriate; the next booking(s), including any requirements for equipment so that the booking system can be kept current; a note of the actual materials being worked on so that they can be reserved if necessary. How detailed this needs to be depends on what the centre's responsibility is. If it just has to make sure the relevant resources are available, the record can be a simple form; if it has also to monitor the student's progress and to provide support and guidance, then the record needs to be a folder with room for recording not only attendance, etc but progress, results of assessments, etc.

3. A control catalogue of available materials and equipment, so that the administration always knows:

a) what it has
b) the age, status, condition of each item (for stock control)
c) availability or non availability (eg because of booking).

All these may sound cumbersome but, once set up, ease operation enormously. Moreover a hidden implication of all this is that the centre may have to justify itself, or at least show what use is being made of the facilities. It may even have to fit into existing administrative norms (eg for education, calculations of SSRs, problems of double counting of internal students). In this case some sort of time/body register may have to be devised since, except in group workshops, students may not attend in tidy, hour-sized bites. Here it is worth remembering that x students in a room, albeit doing different things, can nonetheless be equivalent to a class of x students over the same period. Thus it may be useful to employ either a block register showing occupancy regardless of names or else one based on Mackay's concept of the serial class in which individual student attendances are logged irrespective of particular time periods; examples are shown in Appendix 3.

Client monitoring
If the centre is responsible for its students, then it has to meet one or both of two needs:

a) To report at intervals to an external sponsor who is finally responsible for the student's progress.

b) To help/guide/assess the student who uses the service as the core of his or her learning.

Where the traditional open learning concept of each student having a personal tutor is followed, then that tutor can be tasked with keeping the student's record up-to-date and generally taking responsibility. That may, however, not be the case: a student may come in to carry out a short piece of work for which no formal tutoring is required; the personal tutor system may not be appropriate for all sorts of reasons and, in any case, cost or possible inconvenience may need to be weighed against other methods. In such cases, the centre will need to keep detailed records of work so that someone else advising later on can see what has gone before

- continuity needs to be established.

It is, therefore, sensible for 'continuing' students (ie those following a course) to have a detailed folder which includes notes on progress, assessments, etc as well as a record of attendance. In many cases most of the entries can be made by the student but it should be retained at the centre or workshop. Most usually such records are paper-based but it is worth remembering that any computerised ones need to comply with the provisions of the Data Protection Act.

There is also a need for everyone concerned to know exactly what the procedures are: who checks the student's progress, who is responsible for arranging any examinations or external assessments.

Liaison and marketing
This is where effective administrative procedures prove their worth. Unlike a general-use facility such as a library, a learning facility *must* be au fait with how each of its clients is progressing; when called on, or when its staff recognise the need, the centre must be in a position to counsel and guide the individual students effectively and to show any sponsors that it is being effective. It is quite often difficult initially to convince those outside - whether they be teaching departments or company sections - that such facilities can be positive helps rather than threats to an established order or just ways of wasting time.

One way is to show that the centre, like a certain beer, can 'reach parts that other provision does not reach'. Look to offer help to students who, for some reason have had to miss out on parts of their education or training; find out if, by using flexible learning methods - especially structured packages - the range of student options in a certain course might be extended; see if the increasing trend towards modularisation offers alternative paths through a programme of work. Could centre provision enable the institution to offer service to small groups that would not otherwise be economically viable? Mixed-mode courses may well have a part to play, both in education and training as numbers of young people decrease and small quantitities of adults must be re-trained. How can flexible learning be built into such courses and how can the centre help?

81

If a centre/workshop can once demonstrate these uses then it is on the way to being accepted and integrated - and if it cannot do so, then why was it initiated at all? The point to get over is that the workshop/centre approaches can enhance the provision others are making, rather than replace it. This point is usually taken from the start by subject workshops because of their origins, though they often do not take the logical step of looking beyond their original purpose to other things they could offer. Generalist centres, including specialised training facilities in big firms, on the other hand, often do not recognise that potential customers (as sponsors of students) may see them as rivals, if their position is not made clear.

Plant and stock control

The implications of these for centre management are that they have to be done, otherwise chaos will eventually ensue! The equipment will, presumably, be held on some form of inventory in any case but there are good reasons to keep a card (or computer) index for each item, recording its vital statistics (serial; date of purchase; source; amortised cost if needed) and providing a record of repairs and availability.

Stock, in the form of the learning materials, also needs control so that at any time the centre knows what it has available, where it is and when the stock needs replenishing. This is particularly so in the case of worksheet or assignment materials where suddenly finding out that the supply has run out does nothing for morale! The sensible approach is to keep these filed in batches and to put a reminder tag - a coloured sheet of paper or something similar - ten or so copies before exhaustion point as a hint to get some more run off. More complex packages can best be served by a simple stock card system and, in the writer's experience, there is little advantage in computerising that - a card is much quicker to glance at if properly filed.

Stock control is also vital because learning packages, by their nature, are not long-life items like library books or media resources. Even if they have been designed to be reusable, accelerated usage will mean that paper-based items probably will not survive more than five or six handlings before disintegrating (after all they are being constantly thumbed and referred back and forth unlike the average book) so that they will need constant replacement (see chapter 3 for cost implications). Many so-called reusable packs actually achieve this by including consumable workbooks, etc, which may need regular restocking. Others are either 'one-shot' items by design or you may wish to sell copies on. In all these cases accurate stock records and regular checks are vital.

Last but not least, there is an increasing tendency to reduce materials cost to the student by either loaning (against a deposit) or renting out packages if the student wants to work elsewhere. The centre management will then have to decide how such stocks are to be provided and depreciated and also establish a recording system for handling loans and rentals; probably the existing library system can handle the job but it will need to be arranged.

The last implication of stock control for learning facilities is, perhaps, the most important: what are the sources of supply and how can one get some indication of the material's quality as a *learning* package? There is as yet little really useful formal evaluative information widely available, so Appendix 2 give you a do-it-yourself form to build up your own information bank. As to outside suppliers, the alternatives are to look up individual materials producers in various directories and maintain a register of negotiations with them, or to use one of the regional delivery agencies which sprang, mostly, from the former MSC's Open Tech Project. These, in effect, act as middlemen, all publishing some sort of catalogue and usually offering some form of discount on retail prices, though you may have to shop around. Their advantages are that you can usually place all your orders at once with a single agency and they may be prepared to send inspection copies which few producers are currently willing to do. Their disadvantages are those of any commercial organisation in that, the more self-sustaining they need to be, the less objective they can be about their products; a limited range of items offering a high rate of return is clearly more desirable for them than a wide spread of low cost items so you must expect them to 'push' certain wares - but then so will any producer recommend his own stock. Those agencies run by or through LEAs with some form of subsidy are likely to be the most objective and informative but their services may not be available outside their own areas.

Useful References

Davies, W J K, *Alternatives to Class Teaching in Schools and Colleges* (Guidelines 9),CET, 1980. Chapter 10 gives guidance on administration and monitoring procedures.

Lewis, R, *How to Develop and Manage an Open Learning Scheme* (Open Learning Guide 5), CET, 1985. Section 2 of this guide is particularly useful since many of its aids apply to both distance and centre-based operations.

Lewis, R and MacDonald, L, *The Open Learning Pocket Workbook*, NCET, 1988. A summary of checklist information from the various CET Open Learning Guides, this is a useful aide-memoire although biased to 'traditional OL'.

Marshall, I, *Training Course in Delivery of Open Learning Schemes Pts 1-3*, SCOTTSU, 1987. Although concentrating on distance learning, this open learning package is very useful and practical, especially Pt 3 'Managing an OL Scheme'.

Rowlands, N and S, *Into Open Learning*, Open Learning Systems Ltd, 1986. A useful practitioners' guide with helpful advice and forms for OL deliverers, particularly those running workshops.

Materials supply
MARISNET, The Old Bank House, Ely, Cambs. This is a computerised database service offering on-line information to subscribers. It claims to have over 7,000 items on call but is unselective; no quality control or other evaluation information about the items is currently available.

National Open Learning Association: a grouping of producers, delivery systems and users of open/flexible learning. Information about its members can be obtained from the secretary, currently situated at: Eastek, High Street, Hadleigh, Suffolk.

Open Learning Directory: published annually on behalf of the Training Agency (formerly Training Commission), this lists a large proportion of the useful UK-produced material.

8. USING THE FACILITY AND MANAGING THE LEARNING

'But who has won?' asked Alice.
'Everybody has won' said the Dodo
- Alice in Wonderland

'He can't see the wood for the trees' - English proverb

How one manages the actual learning that goes on through any given learning facility really depends on the reasons for, and the nature of, the provision. Why did the facilities come into existence and is there a thought-out corporate view on what they are going to be used for? How will they affect the great mass of curriculum provision within the institution - and this affects both education and industry; is a 'learning centre' in a training department, for example, to be the focus of its work or is it intended as a useful extra? Or take the example of a subject workshop: some institutions simply make it available as a facility; others fill it by 'converting' taught courses to individualised work; a few venturesome places have taken up variants of contract work in which all or most of the Maths courses have been modularised but each student has a great deal of control over how, when and in what order the work is completed.

Does it matter and should the institution have a policy on this when it considers setting up a learning centre in macro terms? The answer must be that, yes, it does matter in that the policy, whether tacit or explicit, may well affect both viability and the degree of continuing involvement at institutional level. If, for example, a Mathematics workshop is perceived by its sponsors as being largely for individualised GCSE courses, with anything else being extra, that will tend to determine both the staff allocation and the flexibility of use. Equally, if a generalist learning room is seen mainly as providing a set of discrete, package-based modules, its possible uses in the development of course-length provision may be ignored. In both cases the institutional management may feel that, since the original aims have been met, the initiative can just plod on; thus no further thought is given to developing and extending (or reducing) its work.

Let us, therefore look at various aspects of actually using the facility and what their implications are for curriculum approaches and for managing the learning that takes place subsequently in or through the facility itself.

The major purposes and, hence, uses of the organisation we are calling a learning centre can be one or more of the following:

Replacing specific taught courses by individualised work, in whole or part;

Building-in extra options not otherwise viable;

Developing new courses and options;

Modifying the total curriculum approach of either a section or the whole of the institution.

The first three tend to be initiated from the bottom, up; that is to say that individual sections - or even individuals - can develop them comparatively easily and without more than minimal sponsorship by the institution as a whole. The fourth has to be initiated as a result of cross-institutional discussion and decisions at top management level - revolution rather than evolution, so to speak. It therefore is likely to have much more significant effect on how the learning is managed.

Equally, although people tend to have a preconceived idea about what they want from a particular initiative, it is always worth remembering that there are at least four parallel functions which a centre might encompass, and the more of them involved the more flexible and useful the provision is likely to be. Managing the learning in it is also likely to get progressively more difficult but we will deal with that below! Meanwhile the suggested functions are:

a)   *Remedial:* either making the facilities available as needed, or deliberately structuring them in order to pick up students who, for some reason, have fallen behind with work or have gaps in their competences.

b) *Supplementary:* providing extra options that would not otherwise be viable (for example enabling small-number groups to be accommodated) or extending depth of provision in a given subject area.

c) *Replacement:* of taught courses by individualised and other flexible learning approaches (ie actually deliberately changing the instructional strategy).

d) *Creation (of new opportunities):* providing new courses or modules not taught conventionally and thus extending the educational or training curriculum available.

All, except possibly the last, imply that there has already been some rethinking going on in that, to be successful, they require existing courses and provision to have been modularised. In this context, this means that they have been so examined that given areas of learning have been analysed into their component parts, the relationships between those parts established with any options or variant routes identified, and suitable assessment devices provided to check progress.

If a centre is to be used effectively, indeed, modularisation implies even more than this. A teacher or instructor, in a group lesson, can so organise his work that the students perceive that lesson as a whole, a coherent unit of learning which has both a beginning and an identifiable break-point at its end. A student working by self-study, unless he or she is very well organised, expects the learning material, whether package or work-sheet, to perform that function for him; ie it will be so structured that, in the allocated time period, it will cover a coherent piece of learning and draw it to a 'natural break'. Thus the work not only needs to be modularised but the modules need to be divided into handy bite-sized chunks which will not leave the student half-way through and 'hanging in the air' when the time comes to stop. Otherwise, not only does he lose his train of thought but he takes an unnecessarily long time picking it up again on his next visit - two steps forward and one back rather than three steps forward.

This has two implications for managing the learning. The centre staff must, so far as possible, match student with material and time, not just with material; and the materials designer or buyer must take this into account when organising such materials for use in a centre environment.

It therefore has considerable practical implications for the provision of what the jargoneers like to call 'learning experiences' - for us the actual quanta of self-study that a student undertakes at one sitting. To illustrate this, we can take an analogy the writer has found helpful, that of the learning country. Assume that to reach any one of a number of goals or destinations, our students have, in effect, to get across a stretch of previously unknown terrain in which they can easily get lost. The conventional method is for the travel agent (teacher or instructor) to act as a tour operator. He decides on the most effective goal and route, puts thirty or so students in a bus or train and takes them across as a group (without being too cynical, the main change in recent years is that he might use the bus because it does allow a number of different routes). Modularisation of such a scheme basically identifies meal stops and overnight places and builds them into the programme with some possible optional excursions.

The development of student-centred approaches, however, means that our travel agent has to change his role since he no longer accompanies and directs the student traveller. Instead, he maps the country to find the different interesting routes, identifies points of difficulty and then provides the student with a detailed guidebook, in asssimilable sections, to help him on his way. In a traditionally tutored system, the guide includes a 'helpline' either as a contact literally by phone or as a series of assignation points which the student, hopefully, reaches to find his friendly travel agent has mysteriously appeared to set him on the next stage; how reassuring - provided the student does not fall by the way-side. A 'centre-based' concept takes that one stage further in that it assumes there will always be knowledgeable inhabitants about who can answer queries and provide guidance. . . and that is the crunch point. These inhabitants do not actually need to know the student's guidebook in detail (ie they do not need to be totally familiar with a given package) since they know the country itself but they do need to know the lunch stops, the breaks and the possible permutations of routes at each junction.

This must have definite implications both for learning design and for the actual management of it. First, the area of knowledge, skill, etc concerned must have been genuinely modularised in advance: that is coherent parts must have been identified, of an appropriate study size and with their links to other parts clearly shown. The latter is vital because, just as leaving a learner 'hanging' half-way through is bad practice, so is giving him chunks of learning that are so discrete that the learner cannot connect them up or see their relevance to the whole.

Secondly, the modularisation plan must be translated into terms that the individual learner can recognise. The content of individual modules must be matched across with learning materials, whether these be commercially published, home-grown or simply guidelines. This can be difficult especially with existing packs because they may not have been structured with your needs in mind or, even if they have, a single pack may incorporate several modules. That is sometimes a real argument for designing your own materials, so long as you also take the time factor into consideration!

Implications for Managing the Learning
Firstly, centre personnel need to recognise that, given a chance, individuals learn at different rates and, to some extent, in different ways. Where possible, therefore, the facility's timetable should not be so rigid as unduly to restrict a learner's study period. Unless modules are very short, this does tend to work against conventionally timetabled groups simply converting to worksheet learning. Where possible in such cases, it is desirable to see if the course can be so structured that learners have control over how they proceed. They may, for example, simply be given a block of work to carry out over a period of several weeks using some variant of the contract system, while their progress may be monitored by their course tutor.

Secondly, personnel need either to know materials in outline or to have access to information about the study time of each item. They also need to be able to check with learners that the learner knows what he is taking on and actually to supervise the work to ensure so far as possible that it does finish at a natural break.

Thirdly, the staff, or some of them, will increasingly have to be aware of the needs of external accreditation. They may have to be able to arrange examinations, or at least to liaise with the institution's examinations section, since some of the qualifications towards which students are working may not currently be on the institution's books. Moreover, with the increasing emphasis towards competency-based work in education and training, they may well have to act as assessors from time to time.

Fourthly, the staff need to be aware that their role is changing. Obvious, you say - they become tutors not teachers. Everyone knows that! The writer would suggest, however, that even this shift is no longer entirely valid and its retention may, indeed, be contributing to some of the perception problems flexible learning is experiencing. In a centre or workshop context, the staff manning the facility are often in yet a third role, that of learning adviser or consultant. That is to say they may not have personal responsibility for an individual student but are there to sort out problems for anyone who asks and to guide students as required. They may, in some cases, not even know the totality of what a particular student is doing; in our learning country analogy they are knowledgeable inhabitants who can point the student in the right direction for the next meal stop and help him sort out any difficulties in getting there.

There are also many occasions when such staff may also have an intermediate role, for example when a learner is doing something which may require feedback to an external teacher or trainer. In such cases, the centre staff may need to monitor more closely and tell others what they have advised.

Lastly, the staff may indeed be in the role of tutor but one in which they see 'their' students frequently but fleetingly - for brief checks on progress during centre visits, as part of a group in a periodic seminar, on demand at a regular surgery - rather than occasionally but in depth. The writer would suggest that, if flexible learning is to become widespread, this is no bad thing; an independent traveller who can pick his route in the knowledge that problem-solving help is always around is likely to end up more confident in future than one who is either mollycoddled or whose help is unnaturally restricted to a few given times. In the old programmed learning days there used to be a joke society for helping to stamp out small steps which were regarded as the bane of the method. Perhaps, in developing flexible learning, we need a serious attempt to help stamp out the teaching tutor!

Useful References

Davies, I K, *The Management of Learning*, McGraw Hill, 1971. This is still the best general text on the theory and practice of learning management.

Davies, W J K, *Implementing Individualised Learning*, CET, 1978. Much of this is now dated but the advice on planning learning activities and designing work materials is still relevant.

Waterhouse, P, *Managing the Learning Process*, McGraw Hill, 1983. A book intended mainly for schools, this still has some useful general advice, especially on the management of individual and small group learning (chapter 7).

9. PULLING IT ALL TOGETHER

'Five Workshops - four and the one we don't mention'
- With apologies to 'Salad Days'

We have had a look at all the important detailed aspects of learning centres as facilities. Now it is time, perhaps, to come back to where we left off at the end of chapter 2 and think again about just how and why (and perhaps even whether) we might get involved with the concept in practice.

The evidence so far is that, if enthusiast generated, most workshops or learning centre initiatives will work up to a point; it is where an institution moves from Topsy-led development to institution-planned schemes - ie moves towards revolution rather than evolution - that the true divide comes. At that point, there are some models that appear to have greater potential for development than others and some which, although attractive in the short term, are unlikely to have much long-term potential at all. Almost any single facility will have more limited scope for development than a related group because of limitations on size and the likelihood that it will be sectional in interest but it does not necessarily follow that a collection of facilities will do better. It is the institution's perception as a whole that counts.

Let us have a look at several models to illustrate these points. The most obvious one is that of a college of further education which sets up a home study scheme based on the (student + package + personal tutor) formula. While in no way denigrating the usefulness of this approach for some students, its cost and the problems of providing a satisfactory service at a reasonable price make it difficult to develop. Add to this the fact that, from all the evidence, there is a limited market for such provision and it is difficult to see how it can ever become more than peripheral *on its own*. It may, indeed, dwindle away to 'the one we don't mention' even if there is other flexible learning provision. Its industrial equivalent, where the employer hopes employees will in effect train themselves in their own time, may have slightly more success because the reward for student achievement is usually more obvious but it still has the same weaknesses.

Again, the obvious development, where an institution provides a drop-in or ' by appointment' centre to counter-balance the distance learning element, has so far tended to run into the same problems. This is not so much because of cost - as discussed in chapter 2 this can be quite reasonable - but because:

a) The origins of many such facilities lie in the belief that they were needed because distance students required to use specialist equipment; hence they tended to be extra facilities in the sense of technical workshops rather than learning bases.

b) They have tended to be seen as an extra provision and, therefore, one which is expected to earn all or most of its income. Thus in education there is a thrust towards bringing in new clients rather than providing services for the institution itself (which cannot overtly be charged). Industrial drop-in facilities tend to avoid this problem, it is true, because they are for internal use.

Such centres can prove quite viable within these terms of reference and some, indeed, have a very high profile and are cited as successful. This is quite true *but* their problem is that they have little development potential for the institution as a whole. Until the institution deliberately incorporates the facility into its own work and makes resource provision to do so, it will not get widely involved and the initiative will have little impact on the overall curriculum. Here again, the strictures do not apply so much to in-house training centres because of their internal usage.

Thirdly, there is the model of a single subject workshop set up initially to serve specific purposes - for example to individualise GCSE courses. That, one might say, potentially has development potential. Its difficulty may well be that, because of its origins, its staff have doubts about taking other activities on board and its sponsors may have organisational problems within the institution if they want to expand the range of work. Thus its development is often hampered not so much by the possibilities but by the patterns of thought that gave it birth.

The acid test is to ask whether the facility(s) could be closed down with little or no effect on the main work of the institution. The first two are unlikely to qualify for survival on these terms, the third will only do so if it extends its work so that all or much of the tuition in that subject area depends on using the workshop approach; that, in effect, it has by evolving, achieved a mini-revolution.

All these models have something in common: they are examples of isolated facilities more or less turned in upon themselves - sufficing within their own frameworks but doing no more.

Such evidence as there is indicates that only where there are multiple facilities or facilities that have multiple reasons for existence will consid-erable development - and corresponding usefulness to the institution - take place. There probably is good reason for the early initiatives being in such areas as Maths and Communications for they are common to most courses within an institution's provision. A common core can be helpful, even on a small scale, if it proves the usefulness of the concept beyond a single section or department. Equally, multiple facilities, if they are co-ordinated so that there is effective access to all of them, can be a very effective means of increasing flexibility beyond their individ-ual capacities - provided there is an institution-wide realisation of their value.

So we come round to the original thesis that, if an institution wishes to adopt a truly flexible approach to learning, it needs to give potential customers the choice exemplified by *figure 1* (page 19). In order to do that, it needs a range of facilities for both group and individual work and a philosophy to match. . . and, in turn, that means formulation of a coherent policy at institutional - or at the least, at major section - level in order to provide the ways and means. If it is starting from scratch, this may not be so difficult - even if the decision is to start development in one area that will be recognised as having wider-than-local value and can be designed for incorporation in wider schemes if and as they eventuate. To redevelop from an existing enthusiast generated initiative is more problematical but it is undoubtedly worth making the effort even at the expense of some initial disturbance; otherwise that initiative may well become 'the one we don't mention' in any future institutional scheme. It is the writer's hope that this little book may at least help in avoiding that pitfall.

APPENDIX 1: STAFFING FOR FLEXIBLE LEARNING

Staffing for flexible learning schemes is needed on three levels:

a) Co-ordination, to be undertaken by an individual at senior level and/or by a co-ordinating group with allocated responsibilities.

b) Facility management, to be undertaken normally by a responsible member of staff allocated full or part time as a facility (centre or workshop) manager.

c) Facility staffing, including administrative and tuitional, who may undertake supervision, processing and guidance.

The appendix is divided into two parts: job/task priorities (because too often too many jobs are lumped together), and job descriptions for each level.

Suggested Priorities for Postholders in a Flexible Learning Scheme
Note 1: It is assumed that the main jobs are carried out by different people. Where there is only one learning facility, the tasks of the co-ordinator/facility manager must, perforce, be combined and one or more of the centre staff may have to take on some management functions.

Note 2: The intention is to indicate workload balance. It is suggested that the priorities are ranked as follows:

1. Major tasks/responsibilities.
2. Secondary tasks/responsibilities (assistance/supervision).
3. Only to be done in an emergency (ie not routine parts of the job).
0. Not applicable to this post category.

A. Management/Development Functions (institution and facility level)

Task Level	Co-ordinator		Facility Mgr		Staff/Tutors
	Inst	Facy	Inst	Facy	Facility
Overall responsibility	1	2	3	1	0
System supervision	1	2	3	1	2
Staffing - selection	1	1	2	1	0
- allocation	1	2	2	1	3
Admin - general	1	2	3	1	2
- students	2	3	2	1	1
Finance	1	2	3	1	2
Marketing	1	2	2	1	0
Development	1	1/2	2	1	3
Liaison	1	1	2	1	2

B. Tuition Functions (relating to students at facility level)

Functions	Co-ordinator	Facility Mgr	Staff/Tutors
Responsibility	2	1	2
Enrolment/counselling	3	1	2
Supervision	0	2	1
Tutoring/guidance	0	3	1
Accreditation	2	1	2
Administration/processing	0	1	2

C. Materials Functions

Functions	Co-ordinator	Facility Mgr	Staff/Tutors
Evaluation	1	2	2
Selection	1	1	3
Purchase	1	2	0
Maintenance	0	1	2
Development/production	1	1	0

Job Descriptions for Postholders in Flexible Learning Schemes

A. Co-ordinator/Co-ordinating Group

Advise and assist institution management in:

1. Drawing up and implementing internal policies on flexible learning.
2. Designing, equipping and maintaining appropriate facilities.
3. Devising and agreeing costing and charging structures and instruments.
4. Devising and carrying out staff development in and by flexible learning techniques.
5. Promoting and marketing flexible learning internally and externally.
6. Developing the use of flexible learning as appropriate for the institution.

Undertake and be responsible for management of flexible learning, specifically:

7. Preparation and control of the learning centre's budget where appropriate.
8. Local management of externally funded projects.
9. Overall allocation of tasks and responsibilities to learning centre staff.
10. Training and overall supervision of learning centre staff.
11. Overall management and supervision of flexible learning facilities (workshops, etc).
12. Overall arrangements for external assessments and for accreditation of learners.
13. Selection and purchase of learning materials.
14. Co-ordination of design/development/production of internally produced materials.
15. Liaison with internal and external customers (student sponsors).

B. Facility Manager

Advise and assist the co-ordinator/co-ordinating group in:

1. Development of the facility as a part of the institutional provision.
2. Evaluation and extension of material stocks.
3. Marketing the services of the facility.
4. Development and integration of facility-specific materials.

Undertake and be directly responsible for:

5. Day-to-day allocation of staff tasks/responsibilities.
6. Supervision of staff and students.
7. Timetabling and student scheduling.
8. Administration and record keeping.
9. Day-to-day financial transactions.
10. Maintenance of the facility (accommodation, stock, etc).
11. Supervision of assessment and accreditation procedures.
12. Liaison with co-ordinator/co-ordinating group.

C. Facility Staff (manning during opening hours)

Undertake/be responsible for:

1. Prompt, effective handling of student queries.
2. Supervision and guidance of students.
3. Administration of facility procedures (bookings, etc).
4. Student record keeping.
5. Administering assessment/accreditation procedures.
6. Assessing learners' needs and devising appropriate programmes of work.

APPENDIX 2: ASSESSMENT OF METHODS

Materials Evaluation   **Package Assessment Proforma**
Notes for Package Assessors

These notes are intended to help you complete package assessments in a way that may be useful to others. The form is in three parts each designed to be issued separately if needed (hence the slight overlap of information). With the advent of modularisation, I have built in a section on that which may be useful in the near future.

FRONT PAGE: This is simply guidance to help you clarify your overall opinion but does show any reader at a glance what features the package does or does not have.

FLEXIBLE LEARNING PACKAGE ASSESSMENT PROFORMA: FRONT PAGE

Assessor:	2nd opinion:

Package title:

Publisher:

Supplier's Ref:	Retail Price:

Format:

PACKAGE ASSESSMENT: INITIAL CHECKLIST

1. Does the package title accurately reflect its contents? (If not, note and suggest one)	YES/NO
2. Does the package have stated objectives? 2a. IF NOT, can you deduce them from information given?	YES/NO YES/NO
3. Does it have a stated study length? (If so, please note it here: ....hrs)	YES/NO
4. Does it have a stated audience/study level that is useful to you?	YES/NO
5. Does it contain recommendations for support?	YES/NO
6. Does it have in-built assessment instruments? (SAQs with answers; tutor assignments, etc)	YES/NO
7. Will further assessment need to be provided for any accreditation?	YES/NO
8. Can the package conveniently be split into sections for practical use?	YES/NO
9. IF SO, can you group these as short units of study?	YES/NO
10. Does the package contain any self-evaluation?	YES/NO
11. Does the package include a study guide for the learner?	YES/NO
12. Does the package include a tutor's guide?	YES/NO

OVERALL ASSESSMENT (based on checklist answers)   CIRCLE BOXES

GOOD;	ADEQUATE;	NEEDS ADAPTATION;	NOT RECOMMENDED;	SCRAP;
FREE-STANDING;		USABLE 'AS IS';	NEEDS EXTRA SUPPORT;	

Usable as:	SINGLE MODULE;	PART OF MODULE;	SEVERAL MODULES;

MAIN FORM: Notes on possible ambiguities follow.

AUDIENCE: We have problems in defining the potential audience and purpose for a package. This is an attempt to do so but you may wish to add others.

LEVEL: This is free text to allow assessors to make a value judgement. Entries could be a qualification level (eg GCSE) or a straight indication (eg Basic Skills).

LENGTH: What the package recommends in terms of study hours.

STUDY UNITS: Try to see if the pack can be split into workable units of study, about 2 to 3 hours in length each, at most.

EQUIPMENT: Note in detail any needs (eg IBM compatible micro with 5 1/4 inch disc drive).

SUPPORT: Note what the package recommends. If you wish to differ, make clear they are your views.

EXTERNAL QUALNS: Some packages are 'approved' for national qualifications. List these where appropriate.

MODULAR APPLICATIONS: I suspect we shall all find it helpful soon if we have this information so why not start now? The title should be as specific as possible and it will help if you can indicate what, if any, extra assessment would be needed for external accreditation. The last section is put in because a package may not match a syllabus section exactly.

OBJECTIVES: Either use or summarise package objectives if they are stated; otherwise deduce and formulate your own.

ASSESSMENTS: Include such things as SAQs, assignments, etc.

MATERIALS EVALUATION:	OPEN LEARNING MODULE DESCRIPTOR		
FILE REF:		DATE:	REVIEWER:

Package Title	— — — — — — — — — — — — — — — — — — — — — — — — — — — — — — — —
Order Ref:	
Subject Area:	
Audience:	Operative; technician/clerical; admin; supervisory; teacher/trainer; management
Level:	— — — — — — — — — — — — — — — — —
Study Length:	— — — — — — — —
Study Units:	Qty: Unit length:
Equipment Needed:	— — — — — — — — — — — — — — — — — — — — — — — — — — — — — — — —
Suggested Support:	— — — — — — — — — — — — — — — — — — — — — — — — — — — — — — — — — — — — — — — — — — — — — — — — — — — — — — — — — — — — — — — — — — — — — — — — — — — — — — — —
External Qualns:	— — — — — — — — — — — — — — — — — — — — — — — — — — — — — — — —

MODULAR APPLICATIONS (It may be possible to use this package as a module in mainstream FE. Suggested details are below.)

Course(s):	— — — — — — — — — — — — — — — —
Module Title:	— — — — — — — — — — — — — — — —
Possible Ways of Use:	— — — — — — — — — — — — — — — — — — — — — — — — — — — — — — — — — — — — — — — — — — — — — — — —
Accreditation Needs:	— — — — — — — — — — — — — — — — — — — — — — — — — — — — — — — —
Usable as:	SINGLE MODULE; PART OF MODULE; SEVERAL MODULES

DRAFT OPEN LEARNING MODULE DESCRIPTOR: FILE REF:

Package Title: _____

Publisher: _____

Objectives: _____

Pre-entry
Needs: _____

Content
Summary: _____

Inbuilt
Assessments: _____

Additional Information: (NB this may include a personal overall opinion of the package, or part package, as appropriate)

_____

APPENDIX 3: ORGANISATIONAL AIDS

All facilities need the following items:

1) Accommodation plan.
2) Bookings ledger or computer file.
3) Student registration documents.
4) Student booking cards.
5) Student record documents for centre use.

It is also desirable to have:

6) Manual or sheet of staff procedures.
7) A guide leaflet for students.

It appears pointless to replicate existing work and readers are therefore referred to two specific publications containing examples of documentation together with helpful advice. These are:

Davies, W J K, *Alternatives to Class Teaching in Schools and Colleges* (Guidelines 9), CET, 1980. Chapter 10 gives an organisational portfolio with examples of staff procedures and student monitoring documents for centre use.

Rowlands, N and S, *Into Open Learning*, Open Learning Systems Ltd, 1986. This has a lot of useful forms and procedures scattered through it.

This appendix contains ideas for the administration documents most needed to get a facility up and running.

Booking Arrangements

1) Accommodation plan. This should show the layout diagrammatically with each workstation identified by a number (repeated physically on the station itself) and a code for any special fittings. Different facilities will have different needs but it is suggested a wipe-clean board is used so that occupancy at any given time can be seen at a glance.

2) Booking ledger (or computer file). This should be linked directly to the plan by station references and maintained about a month in advance. It should then enable 'reception' to identify quickly if a slot is vacant or not.

3) (Optional but useful.) A 'blow-up' of the current day's booking sheet for instant reference by all. Until recently, a wipe-clean board would have been recommended but enlarging photocopiers can do the job more speedily!

BOOKING DOCUMENTS

1.

Code:

M = micro

E = fitted with
    electric point(s)

V = video

2.

DAY				
Times				
Stations	9 30	10 00	10 30	11 00
1 (VHS video)				
2				
3				
4				
5 (VHS video)				
6				
7				
8 IBM PC				

Student Booking Documents

1) Issue each student with a pass. There are many ways of doing this but a convenient one is a folded-A5 booklet with a double page for each facility (if there is more than one). The sketches are self-explanatory.

2) Keep a record equivalent at the centre. This could be a simple photocopy of the pass or the modification seen here which performs a rudimentary monitoring function.

Records of Attendance *(see diagrams on page 112)*
Attendance can be recorded in various ways to allow for the flexibility variables. Three are shown in the diagram:

a) Recording number of attendances over a given period for accounting purposes. If the institution simply needs to know occupancy it can be done like this.

b) Recording irregular attendances by individuals with freedom to come at times convenient to themselves. The 'length' column is there because some institutions have found a need to allocate periods of time in their records.

c) Recording essential contacts (eg for accreditation purposes). This is particularly useful for distance learning students.

STUDENT BOOKING DOCUMENT

1a)

OPENING TIMES	LOAMSHIRE COLLEGE
Maths Wshp (Room 12) M-Th 9.00-3.00 Fri 9.00-12.00	**Flexible Learning Student Pass**
Learning Centre M-Fri 9.00-8.00	
Library M-Fri 9.00-8.00	Session.................... Name......................

Facility identified   *For admin use to record attendence*   *Address or internal contact*

b)

NAME					CONTACT	
WKSHP		DATE ISSUED				
Date	Times	Wk Stn	Chk		Work Programme/Package	

Start and finish if possible   *Enough info to identify exactly*

2

NAME		CONTACT	
WKSHP			
Date	Work to do	Work completed	Checked?

ATTENDANCE CARDS

To record numbers of attendances

a)

DAY		1	2	3	4	5	6	7	8	
9 - 10		/	/	/	/	/	/	/	/	
10 - 11		/	/							
11 - 12		/	/	/	/					

Could be subdivided or 'part taken as whole'

b)

Name	Date	Length	Date	Length		
ABEL J						
BLOOD V						
CATTERMOLE A						

c)

COURSE	Tutorial 1	Seminar 1	Assgt 1	Assgt 2			
ABEL J							
BLOOD V							
CATTERMOLE A							